ENDORSEMENTS

"An emotional rollercoaster that explores the fears, hopes, and triumphs of one woman's journey through high-risk pregnancy, including the challenges she faces and the support she receives along the way."
- Alana Smiley, Love Team at Grady's Decision

"Shelbi Zimmerman's book is poignant and sweet with a message for anyone going through a hard time- be it with infertility, a life altering diagnosis or any hardship this world may have. When our heads and hearts are discouraged, turn your eyes to the One who made us. When our hopes are failing, Jesus never will. With Him all things are possible and Lincoln is testimony that with a parent's love can move mountains."
- Mary Shaffer RN, Life's Journey OBGYN

"Shelbi and her family's honesty and generosity sharing their truth is as brave as it is powerful. As humans we sometimes have a lifetime with our babies and sometimes precious minutes, but our love for them endures. I hope her experience inspires others to know they are not alone on a less traditional journey to parenthood and to travel their path with authenticity and love."
- Christina Pisani-Conway, MD, Maternal Fetal Medicine Physician, RYT200, RPYT, Ayurvedic Yoga Specialist

"Born for this is a heart-wrenching story that really shows the lengths a mother will go for her child, before and after their entrance into this world. A real and raw story of the struggles of motherhood while showing the power Faith for anyone going through difficult times; whether you are a parent, grieving any type of loss, or simply going through a rough patch in life. It's an addicting, powerful, and inspiring story for all people. The kind of stories we need to be sharing with each other."
- Aryn Gibson, Host of the Momfullness Podcast, and Nurse Midwife in the making

born for this

*Embracing the Journey from
High-Risk to Hopeful*

born for this

*Embracing the Journey from
High-Risk to Hopeful*

SHELBI ZIMMERMAN

Paperback ISBN: 979-8-9885850-6-0
Hardback ISBN: 979-8-988585-0-7

Cover Design and Layout: Katie Zeliger
Cover Photography: Brittany Bowley

Printed in the United States of America
Meraki Press LLC
www.merakipress.org

First Printing, 2024.

To Lincoln
All the strength I have today I owe to you:
my miracle, my hero, my son.

To High-Risk Mothers
May you never feel alone in the dark times
in this journey. May you find great beauty in this pain. Keep
your head up. You were born for this.

TABLE OF CONTENTS

PREFACE

When I found out that I would be facing a high-risk pregnancy, I relied on journaling to get me through it. I wrote this book as a reflection on that period. I knew the one thing that worked for me to process big emotions was writing. I used to write thoughts and then crumple them up– into the trash they went, but journaling during this time was therapeutic. I never wanted to throw away these writings, no matter how hard it was to relive the memories. I gathered my journal entries and pregnancy views from the journey and put together this book for those who need support and a story with which to connect.

Our pregnancy was high-risk. For us, that meant our son had an Omphalocele.

An Omphalocele is a rare congenital birth defect that occurs within the first six to eleven weeks of pregnancy when the fetus's midline and abdomen organ formation and placement occur. There is no known cause for them. Our son's organs grew normally, just like yours and mine.

However, during this process of fetal growth, his organs began to grow, protruding into his umbilical cord, where the belly button would be on his abdomen wall. Those organs did not return to the abdomen but would remain in a transparent sac outside of the abdomen at the location where his belly button should be. Basically, when this congenital birth defect occurs, some of what should remain internal grows outside of the belly wall. Exactly which organs grow externally varies. Omphaloceles occur in 1/ 4,175 pregnancies. Our son had what is called a "giant Omphalocele." Most times, the abnormality shows at the 20-week ultrasound, but we found our son's at the 12-week Nuchal Cord ultrasound by complete chance.

About 50% of babies with Omphaloceles have abnormalities in other organs or body parts. The most common are the spine, digestive system, limbs, heart, and urinary system. About 30% of Omphalocele babies have a genetic abnormality, the most common being Trisomy 13, 18, and 21, Turners Syndrome, or Triploidy.

Some babies have Beckwith-Wiedemann Syndrome. Omphaloceles fall under three categories: small, large, and giant. The categories are in relation to size. Giant Omphaloceles are greater than or less than 5cm. Omphaloceles are more common in males than in females as well.

Some babies are born with an isolated Omphalocele, meaning an Omphalocele with no other congenital disabilities. When an Omphalocele is isolated, the chance for it to reoccur is 1%. If the baby has an isolated Omphalocele, the survival rate is 90%. If the baby has problems with other organs in addition to the Omphalocele, the survival rate is 70%. Babies born with small Omphaloceles are repaired at birth or shortly after delivery; however, Omphaloceles that are larger or that contain more organs are handled with the "paint and wait" method. The paint and wait treatment consists of painting the abdominal sac with iodine to aid in skin growth and healing. Then, the doctors cover it with gauze/ace wraps for compression and wait to see if new skin will grow over the sac. The hope is to render the sac of organs to retract to their place internally and be covered with skin.[1]

INTRODUCTION

Late August 2019

My husband, Dylan, and I got married and hoped to expand our family right off the bat. We were both young and healthy in our twenties, armed with a dreamlike confidence of gliding through a future pregnancy, growing a healthy baby, and strengthening our marriage, friendship, and parenting prowess. Around eight months after our wedding, I took a pregnancy test before heading to work as a school nurse and saw the two pink lines my heart was desperate for.

The nervous excitement was fresh in my mind as I dreamed of the new definition of us. I knew little then that my dream of a smooth road ahead would become a story about a road less traveled. This story would redefine what family, trials, viability, expectations, fear, pregnancy, choice, love, and many more meant to me.

Eight weeks after finding out I was pregnant, we learned that I was high-risk.

Omphalocele. UHM-FA-LO-SEAL, I said to myself repeatedly until the word became numb inside me.

Until that very moment, I'd never known how great the impact of a single word could be.

Omphalocele.

This book is for the 6%-8% of women who are told you have a high-risk pregnancy and for the one in thirty-three who are told, "Your baby has a birth defect." High-risk pregnancies are raw, honest, ugly, and sometimes outright depressing. But they can be so beautiful – full of celebrations, milestones, and hopeful moments.[2]

This book is for the expecting mothers who need a reassuring boost. The highs and lows you feel during pregnancy are constant, expected, and acceptable. You're seen, warrior momma. I wrote this book to encourage first-time parents and anyone going through the thick of a medically complex diagnosis to let themselves go through it all, knowing they're not alone.

This book is an extension of the hope I held onto, even when the doctor's outcomes provided a short supply of it. It's the product of all the things I learned – how to make a mountain out of every small victory, how to permit myself to believe in the unseen more than ever, that perseverance leads to a strength previously untapped, and most of all, that courage is built strongest in the moments of great fear. I wrote this to help mothers stand up for themselves and their unborn children. I found a version of myself that had never existed until my experiences, and I want my fellow mothers to know the journey is not as dark as it may seem.

This book is about not getting the pregnancy you hoped for but the one destined for you and how unmet expectations do not always end in the worst outcomes. It's about you and the life inside you, making the best out of the time you share with your baby, no matter how short or long.

It's about finding hope in the isolation of darkness.

"It is impossible for you to go on as you were before, so you must go on as you never have."

– Cheryl Strayed

CHAPTER 1

Welcome to the Club:
the One That No One Wants to Join

I met Dylan in middle school.

We never had classes together, but I remember seeing him in the hallways and knowing who he was.

It may seem odd, but one of the first things I noticed about him is he had a facial mole similar to mine. It stuck with me, and I thought it looked adorable on him.

We had a high school of over 1,100 students. Our schedules finally collided despite the large class size. I had several boyfriends while our friendship grew, but he always brought a smile to my face more than they did.

We had a lot in common, but the funniest commonality we shared was when we both had broken bones simultaneously. He broke his arm playing football, and I broke my nose playing soccer. Those injuries led us to become close during our swimming class because neither of us was allowed in the water.

During this time, we sat together and completed homework instead. Dylan caught my attention and made me laugh, and I noticed all the work he put in to keep my interest. I still like to jab him about trying too hard.

During the summer, I met him at the local fair. He was there with his family and friends, and I left some friends to hang out with him. We shared a funnel cake, and he introduced me to his dad.

We have a picture from that day that circulated through the family as they retold the story of one of the first girls Dylan *brought around*. All that time, we remained friends, but there was always a spark between us. We never acted on it because I was always in a relationship.

We grew up in each other's orbit through our high school graduation. He attended a trade school for diesel mechanics, and I went to an adult program to obtain my LPN license. We both stayed local.

We met at our old high school's football game one night. Leaving the comfort of the familiar after graduating wore on me more than I expected. Because of the unexpected isolation, I was excited to see someone I knew.

Our typical friendly flirtation seemed different that night. I was newly single, and he was playing *hard to get*. Now, I was the one trying too hard.

We went for ice cream after the game. It would take us some time before we both admitted it, but that night was the kickoff to our relationship (pun intended). We became inseparable over the next few months – talking and texting constantly and living for the weekends.

We each took turns meeting the others' parents and siblings, and in December 2013, we officially became "us."

Early on in our relationship, I had watched him around kids. He appeared so effortless around them.

He was mostly around his cousins' children; that was my first memory of him with any child. Then, as we continued to date, my family expanded, and he would come to interact with my cousins' children, too. We also have always had a friend group a handful of years older than us, and we were always around their children, too.

He was always fun, making up games for them like a cool uncle. It was easy for me to imagine the type of dad he would be one day. I knew we would make a great team – so much so that I was determined to have no less than four children with him when the time came.

In July of 2017, we met up after a friend's baby shower. I saw baby goats walking towards me wearing signs around their necks. One said, "Will you," and the other said, "Marry me?" He was shaking as I yelled "*YES*" through my tears. Our best man wore camo and hid in a bale of hay to record the scene.

Leading up to the wedding, we thought everything was perfect until my dad was in an accident in April of 2018. The resulting injuries affected his ability to walk. My dream of having my father walk me down the aisle was shattered. I tried to envision my first dance with my father, and it made my heart ache, knowing I wouldn't get that special moment.

My father knew how much it meant to me and worked so hard to regain his strength to walk and stand. Eight grueling months later, he was making strides. I began to hope everything I dreamed of could come true once more.

We had a traditional Catholic Mass on our wedding day, December 15th, 2018. The church was full of our loved ones and friends – almost 300 guests. Our colors were navy blue and emerald green, and the bridesmaids wore tartan plaid shawls. The theme was Winter Wonderland, which brought our families together most beautifully. Together, we decked out Christmas trees. His family cooked and catered the most delicious barbecue dinner for our guests. His mother made the cookies, his sister made our wedding cake, and my aunt made our cupcakes and mini cakes for the guests. My mom graciously took on the event manager role, ensuring the entire day flowed seamlessly for me.

It meant so much that my dad could walk me down the aisle eight months after his accident and dance with me at our wedding. These traditions felt monumental to me. Although the weather was rainy and gray, dashing my hopes for a wedding album filled with picturesque scenes and snowy white surroundings. Despite that, the day was perfect.

Once the wedding and honeymoon were over, motherhood was the next hurdle to accomplishing our desired life. We chose to stay in our small town close to our family, hoping our children would have relatives and other children their age to grow up with. We had a huge support system and felt that was an imperative part of becoming parents. Any time one of us had a question too embarrassing to admit we didn't know the answer to, we had friends and family we trusted with the answers. We were glad to plant our roots in the town we knew, in a school system where I worked and so many of my family members also worked.

These hopes were all made before it took almost eight months to conceive. We started the family-expanding process at the end of 2018. We thought we did everything by the book. We were both young and healthy, so I diligently tracked my cycle in various phone apps. Still, each month, when the test read 'negative,' it amplified the previous month's letdowns. The waiting took a toll on us. Early on, we carried that weight individually on our shoulders instead of leaning on each other. We were too afraid of saying – or even thinking – the wrong thing. We were scared of how saying something out loud made a situation real.

Then, one day, I saw a heads-up penny on the floor of our guest bedroom. I had always been in tune with gut feelings and superstitions, and I loved to believe the truth of American Culture that they were simply symbols of prosperity. When I saw the penny, I snatched it up, needing to hold onto the good fortune. I knew at that moment I needed to take another pregnancy test. Despite all the letdowns, this *had* to be a sign from above that it was time. I took the pregnancy test before work, fully expecting it to be negative. I was well prepared for it to be negative yet again. The plus on the wand was a complete surprise. I took another and saw the word *Pregnant*. It appeared very abruptly. The penny flashed to my mind, and I knew deep in my core. *It was a sign from above. It was a win; that good fortune came true!* I put the test in the drawer next to our bed and went to work. Despite the early shock of the day, it was otherwise typical.

When I returned home from work, I went upstairs to change as I usually do. After I changed, I asked Dylan to come upstairs. Maybe something in my voice changed, or I'm just not good at keeping secrets. Either way, he claims to have instinctively known that I was going to tell him we were pregnant. We were both overcome with emotions, but for different reasons. Dylan probably had a mixture of fear, excitement, and anticipation, but I had a barrage of thoughts about the baby being unhealthy. He comforted me, saying I was probably just nervous, and I was hopeful he was right. We decided to celebrate at Dairy Queen.

We decided not to tell anyone until after our first ultrasound to confirm the baby was healthy and had a heartbeat. I knew I desperately needed to tell my mom, so we did while we were eating our Blizzards. Dylan and I were eating ice cream and laughing on the phone with my mother. She was silent on the other end as she was processing the news. It shocked her at first, then she let out a peel of laughter and finally cried. She promised to keep it between us until we were ready to share it with everyone. I was relieved to have someone else to go to with any fear or concerns.

After our first ultrasound, we told our immediate family. We gathered my sisters and dad into our older sister Chelcee's living room to announce the news that I was pregnant and that Mom was able to keep this massive secret for weeks. We were also able to share the news early on that it was a boy because I opted to have bloodwork done. Dylan still laughs, reminding me about how I fell from the recliner to the floor in our old house when I opened the email that said, "Congratulations, it's a boy" and how I cried so much. I was so happy to be having a son and even happier to think of watching Dylan bond with him. At that point, I allowed every hope I had for the future to come to me without reservation.

Our first ultrasound was perfect. I cried, seeing the little blob floating in there with a rapid heartbeat. The word that comes to mind is awe. I was in complete awe that it was really happening, that I had proof he was in there, that we could take a picture of it, that he was ours, and that I was both a mom and becoming a mom. Nothing could take that way. I have to be honest and admit that I also had parallel feelings of worry. I worried and wondered about the changes to my body and our marriage. The way my mind spun joy and fear together from day one is something I think most first-time mothers experience. That day was the first day I felt grateful for my body – for what our bodies can withstand. I also felt empowered in our marriage in the experience of growing a life together while growing in our life together. I understood the gift I'd been given.

Those first few weeks of pregnancy flew by until our twelve-week ultrasound. Seeing the pregnancy test and then seeing our son for the first time all fed the idea that this was real – that it was really happening. But the day we found out our son had an Omphalocele was the true beginning of our shared reality. The important word in that last sentence is *shared*.

I want to acknowledge that many other families endured much more than we did that first year of marriage. At the same time, if I could have done things differently, I would have more intentionally opened the lines of communication with Dylan so that each of us had the prominent other person in their life to share that burden with. The lesson became starkly apparent when we got news about our son's condition. Times like these in life can define a relationship or break it. I am thankful this strengthened us, but the journey to that strength was full of mistakes, hurt feelings, and challenging lessons.

The lessons often led my mind to the image of Dylan and me at the altar on our wedding day. Had I known that day all we would have to face to become the individuals we are, the couple we are, I know I would choose it over and over again. I am grateful we became the mother and father we had to be.

November 14th, 2019

I am 25. Twenty-five, I keep repeating to grasp that I am both young and old enough to be what I am. It's my birthday, and I'm pregnant. Just over twelve weeks along. I am young enough to expect a healthy, uncomplicated pregnancy and old enough to feel equipped to handle the typical throes of parenthood.

But this is not typical. Is it?

Yesterday, my twelve-week scan was abnormal. I almost wish I could say I was surprised. My grandma Edna, who unfortunately passed away before I found out I was pregnant, had what we called magic in her — visions of the future that often came true — an awareness passed down to me. I knew something was wrong from the day I learned I was pregnant, but I prayed it was the usual variety of first-time pregnancy fears. I hoped more than any other time in my life that this time, I was wrong.

We had blood work four weeks ago and learned we are having a boy. Dylan and I were overjoyed. Now, the medical team suggested that we have blood work for a genetic panel to coincide with the nuchal scan we just completed.

Our son appeared to be growing normally. His little hands waved at us on the screen in black and white, his 2mm nuchal cord — perfect. A three-vessel umbilical cord meant he was getting blood and oxygen successfully, and his brain was developing as it should. They showed us the sweetest black-and-white images of his tiny body. But his abdomen was abnormal.

UHM-FA-LO-SEAL. Omphalocele, I keep repeating. Excuse me; what is that?

Dr. Christina asked us how we felt about abortion. It was the easiest no ever decided. It was easier than the yes I said to Dylan when he became my fiance.

November 14th, 2019

The doctor then sat us down while she explained that some of our baby's abdominal organs were outside his abdomen in a sac. At this point, she suspected his liver was not inside his little growing belly. I immediately felt the urge to vomit. I prayed the Serenity Prayer out loud beside Dylan before our appointment that day, not realizing how much we would need those words to carry us through what we were facing.

"Lord, grant me the serenity to accept the things I cannot change, the courage to change the things I can, and the wisdom to know the difference."

Why was I right? How did I know? What did knowing help? My heart lost strength. Nothing will be the same. I stand before a mountain of unknowns, desperate for the next step to reveal itself, drowning in every imaginable scenario. I immediately needed to know the answers, the outcome, the end of this story — a comfort in the nightmare. I feel incapable of overcoming what lies ahead, but at the same time, choiceless in facing it.

The doctor continued explaining the diagnosis, prognosis, and possible outcomes repeating his inquiry: Do you want to terminate?

Do I... what?

How?

Wait, what... no... WHY?

The images flooding my mind went from a future full of bruised knees, college dreams, and bringing home a partner, from first jobs to first heartbreak; all of it dissipated at the uncertainty of this diagnosis.

My dreams for this blossoming life were hiding behind a veil of uncertainty.

November 14th, 2019

The inner turmoil of spinning thoughts read something similar to: This baby can't die — my baby — could die? — before knowing my love? — may never grow out of my stomach — my arms? — may never change the world?

Then it hit me. He already has. This baby has already changed my world. Our world. If I have any say in it, his life will go as follows:

He will be born. He will be loved. He will have surgery, recover, grow healthy, and find success.

Dylan and I decided to move forward without abandoning the hope that brought us to this point.

I sometimes wonder what drove my decision to continue with the pregnancy knowing how hard it would be to sometimes wake up and simply face the days. When I reflect on it, religion and politics were the furthest thing from my mind. While we're Catholic, we're also a Democrat who married a Republican, and those truly weren't even factors for me.

Weighing the true factors of my decision, here's what comes to mind. My husband and I created this child and I would try for him. I knew that if there was even the slightest glimmer of a chance for this child to live I decided to fight as long as he was fighting. He deserved a mama who would choose him.

The heartbeat is the primary sign of life, and my nursing background drilled into me to do no harm. Hearing that heartbeat for the first time was hands down the most breathtaking moment in my life. I believe all lives are deserving of love and a chance to flourish. I was taught in school to fight for a life until the heart gave out. Why should this be any different?

I also had a complete understanding that the pregnancy may not be viable. But I chose to believe that if it were his destiny to pass in utero, then it would occur within the walls of my body, where I would be with him through the end, cradling him both literally and figuratively.

I knew that I had Dylan's support on the matter either way, but the decision to move forward came quickly without discussion. The moment I said yes to moving forward with the pregnancy, I determined that come hell or high water, I would face the unknown outcome. I consented to roll the dice. I agreed to rely on God, myself, my body, and also my baby boy fighting alongside me. I have never felt regret for continuing the pregnancy. I made peace with my decision, hoping it would all come together.

Whether I would have chosen to continue the pregnancy or aid in ending his life was one of the most surreal questions I've ever been asked. No matter the answer chosen, the experience is heartbreaking to face.

In the matter of high-risk pregnancies with a known or unknown fetal diagnosis, there is a quiet grief. Many do not realize the burden of facing the questions around medical abortion. In our case, we were continually asked to terminate up to 32 weeks gestation. It's one thing to make this decision once, but quite another trial to answer it every week for eight months.

Each pregnancy is different, and every mother is unique. Only she can decide what is best for her and her baby. But this fact needs to be talked about more. High-risk mothers are facing excruciating decisions every day.

No matter your opinion on the subject of abortion, until you are placed in the reality of a life-and-death situation that involves your life and now someone else's who relies on you entirely, you can't possibly imagine the internal struggle it is to face. I assure you.

Life has a way of wrecking what you think you want by daring you to show up to your challenges. We left the doctor's office with more than we had asked for. Clinically, our son had a visible midline congenital disability, a bulge in his belly. The doctor ordered aditional labs that would give us a better understanding of the prognosis and next steps.

Dylan and I were shocked and numb on the drive over. The doctor forgot to give us the blood work orders and drove to the lab to hand-deliver them. She sat with us outside the lab to answer any more questions we had. She hugged me and reassured me that she believed he was strong otherwise.

Somehow, I had to find a way to be strong too.

"The world kept turning; I never forgave it for that."

- Ben Breadon

CHAPTER 2

You Can't Strong-Arm Strength

My sister, Chelcee, called me after I texted her that I was getting blood work following the twelve-week nuchal scan. She knew that was a red flag. All I could get out over the phone was, "His liver is not in his body; go to Mom and Dad's." I would have more information to share with her, our parents, and our younger sister, Erika.

I needed a moment to catch my breath. We left the doctor's and headed to the lab. Both Dylan and I were utterly silent. Neither of us had words at that moment. We used the silence to justify our expectations with the reality we now faced. My body was visibly shaking.

When we got to the OBGYN office, the providers hugged us. I didn't have the strength then to receive their compassion; I didn't have the strength to feel anything. They tried their best to reassure us that there would be a solid game plan and that our son looked developmentally healthy otherwise. In those early days, I wanted to wake up from the nightmare. But I knew that it was my reality. *Our* reality.

After our family knew, the most anyone could do was wait. I felt the need to continue with my life, no matter the circumstances or outcome ahead. I didn't want to be unforgiving even as the world continued, as if it didn't just do a complete upheaval upon our lives.

I had to wake up the next day and continue. The rest of the world didn't pause for me to recover from the news. The day after the diagnosis and bloodwork was my birthday. My twenty-fifth birthday. I went to work, and it felt like a better use of my time and weary mind to stick to it. I cooked my birthday dinner and celebrated with Dylan and my sisters. My parents stopped over to visit, and I forced myself to be thankful for what I had.

I did not allow myself time with my thoughts or to catch my breath, and that constant moving forward without letting what happened to be processed started to wreck me.

I felt like I had no choice but to carry on in whatever way I knew how. So, I moved like one who carries a great weight but pretends it's not there, thinking that is what strength looks like.

November 27th, 2019

I'm still sick as hell. I have been sick for two weeks since the news of our son's condition. I am unsure how I held myself together the past fourteen days; my faith has not yet left me. Yesterday morning, Dylan's grandmother passed away. All I could think was how glad I was that she knew about our pregnancy. She already had blankets made for her future grandchildren and gave us several. I am comforted by her unseen future to hope for — something strong to cling to when she passed.

Sunday night, I unleashed my anxiety on Dylan. It came out like anger, but I know it is fear. Sometimes, I forget he is facing this, too. We are both internalizing our struggles with loss. Today, he mentioned that he can't wait for May, the baby's due date. Initially, it made me smile, but I began to cry when he walked away. I cried because I felt ungrateful for what I have now — right now. I cried because it is a blessing to be pregnant. I cried because of hormones, unmet expectations, and probably more reasons I still couldn't find any other way to express. The reminder that happiness could be found amidst this trial — that I had Dylan, our dog, Romo, and our son in our lives.

Our Thanksgiving looked different than I imagined. To white-knuckle myself into a positive outlook, I wore a shirt that said, "Extra thankful this year," and will wear it to announce the pregnancy to our extended families at dinner. I woke up struggling to get dressed overall. It was an extra challenge wearing that shirt. I truthfully didn't intend to wear it at the start of my morning, but I put it on a forced a smile.

Everyone we told about our pregnancy was so happy. I wanted to celebrate with them, but the subsequent excited squeals and offers of congratulations felt like time bombs.

November 27th, 2019

I didn't know what would set me off first: the repeated explanations surrounding the complications of the happy news or the decision not to explain right away to allow the joy robbed from my face to stay on theirs for a bit longer.

I saw the love they had for Dylan and me in that joy. Still, all I wanted to do was sit at the end of the table to announce his diagnosis and our pregnancy plan like a general who discovered the key to world peace:

"Listen up, everyone, this is the diagnosis; these are the statistics. Each month, I'll have one of you work closely with me, someone to make sure Dylan's needs are met, another to cook while we do the hard work of getting this baby stronger, aunties to pray, others to recruit their churches and friends to pray, etc... It's going to take a village to get through this — all hands on deck!"

While internally, I wanted to be in command of my family and their reactions to our pregnancy, I knew I barely had the emotional strength to sit up in my chair that day. I'm glad I didn't attempt control anyway; I would have bawled all day and needed to hold some specifics close until I was more acquainted with them myself. We did ask for prayers, and I requested to withhold further explanation to anyone other than immediate family members.

There are many unknowns ahead. I am scared out of my mind most days. However, I am beginning to believe I can face this and telling myself I will. I'm reminding myself that Dylan and I are already loving parents. I haven't been the best wife through all this, but I am fiercely fighting to be the best mother I can be.

November 27th, 2019

I now pray daily for the confidence to continue on this journey.

I stopped by my grandfather's grave the other day and sobbed. Dylan and I have three lovely grandparents backing us from Heaven while we hold this baby here on Earth. I prayed for them to be with us now as our guardian angels. I have to take each day as it comes. I have to be stronger than I have ever been before.

"Don't give up! I believe in you all; a person's a person, no matter how small."

- Dr. Seuss

CHAPTER 3

Finding My Way Forward: Finding Mothers Like Me

A mixture of emotions lived within me as I stared endlessly at my stomach. There was fear for the health of this life growing inside me, disappointment in being robbed of my perfect pregnancy dreams, anger for how unfair the circumstances of my life felt, and overwhelming love – more love than I thought I could contain. Every step I took through my shattered expectations felt like stepping on the shards of what should be.

Pregnancy hormones are wild. I found myself angry at a *Pampers* commercial. The babies looked healthy, and the mothers looked well-rested. Their expressions showed adoration uncomplicated by fears or messy diapers. My logical brain understood the commercial was staged – that real life was chaotic and complex, but in those early days, I couldn't help but be almost comforted by those bitter thoughts.

After recognizing that the temptation to sink into bitterness was a real possibility, I decided to squash that mindset by researching everything I could find. I needed to find more comfort in what I could control than in what I could not. That research led to an online group called "The MOO Page," or Mothers Of Omphalocele. It was a private group just for moms like me. I submitted a request to join the page after painfully typing out the summary of my story. When the page accepted my request, it unlocked a world of knowledge to parse through but also more uncertainty.

With fetal anomalies, the diagnosis and follow-up testing at the doctor's office were only the starting point. Every time a medical professional told me, "You will know more at birth," my blood pressure would rise. It didn't matter then if it was true – waiting for comfort seemed impossible.

I started to read through the stories on the Mothers Of Omphaloceles page. Everyone's account differed from the rest. I realized my story would, too. It was both helpful and terrifying to see the range of experiences. Some children had comorbidities that complicated their health;

different severities, surgeries, and comorbidities could be associated with children with an Omphalocele.

I even met several families who went through it, and their children had different stories and outcomes. I never met anyone in person, though, for all but one family prior to my delivery, and they quickly became an additional family.

I learned quickly that each family in this group had its own story – that there was no way to predict our son's health and outcome. The only way we would know his Omphaloceles severity and overall health complications would be to wait for the day of his birth. The friends I met online from the page, and I were all due within days of each other.

As I watched their stories unfold, it became clear that this new access to understanding and knowledge had pros and cons.

There were posts offering hope and a positive outlook from real people who seemed like professionals already at tackling their lot in life with grace and the patience of saints. Many parents were willing and gracious to offer their advice and prayers – to walk alongside us so we never had to feel alone. It was also a safe space to express doubts or fears without judgment. People were often gracious and gentle with others, willing to share scenarios and explain their experiences on a parent level instead of a provider level. Simply put, they understood what we were going through.

Despite the pros, the page was a mixed blessing as the cons were at times just as plentiful. Many posts contained losses I was intent on avoiding. Witnessing infant stillbirths and seeing newborns suffer invasive medical interventions such as ECMO and ventilators was intensely challenging as a newly pregnant mother of a child who may face the very same outcomes.

Sometimes, I looked to the page for comfort when my fears crept up, and I would leave the page more defeated than when I logged on. I often begged God to give us time with our son – to know and watch him grow and develop. Other times, my heart went out to parents whose time was cut short and whose outcomes were not what they hoped for.

As my knowledge grew, so did my empathy. Still, I occasionally muted the page when the stories were too much to handle. When I caught myself emotionally investing in every heartbreaking story I saw, I knew I had to remind myself that the page was an important resource. It was too easy to lose myself for hours in this way. I had to protect my baby by learning all I could about his condition, but I also had to protect him by caring for my mental and physical health.

There is nothing wrong with taking time and space when you need it. It is almost necessary for survival to guard yourself from the thoughts and feelings that can easily consume you.

December 6th, 2019

Yesterday was a bad day. I cried often and felt isolated with nothing but my thoughts. The doctors confirmed our son's condition with 100% certainty during the sixteen-week scan. This confirmation ushered me to a new level of grief. Six weeks of being sick has not helped matters. On top of my morning sickness, I have a chest cold — one of the worst I've ever had. I started to feel the baby move around this week. Each movement is a delight. I spoke to the doctor today, and we had a long discussion now that we know more. Our son's liver is the only abdominal organ outside his body. The news brought on an overwhelming sense of peace. I want to cement the hope I have for this baby. He needs a name!

The MOO group (Mothers Of Omphaloceles Facebook Group) has been a true godsend! I now have two women in my back pocket to support me. They each had different outcomes in their experience, but I am so glad to have their support. This little guy will be a fighter, just like their two kids! The women from my group are only towns away! I find myself wishing I had a sense of peace — to feel settled and content in this pregnancy. I am slightly calmer since being told his intestines are still where they need to be.

I want to shift my focus towards my mom's birthday, Christmas, and enjoying the winter season!

I feel the closeness and comfort of my Grandma Edna — like she is guiding me as a calming presence.

"Theology does not become theology until life happens... When we vent, blow up, act out, shake a fist, flip a table, or shut down, God can shape each of these into a part of us so that our experiences sculpt a theology that works... God is no stranger to the dirt. He works best there."

- J.S. Park

CHAPTER 4

A Testimony

During the start of my pregnancy, I was often angry. Knowing something was wrong with my baby and being correct intensified those feelings. I was angry that my baby was not healthy. I was jealous of those who had healthy babies. I was guilt-ridden and, at times, ungrateful for my pregnancy. In my worst moments, I was bitter.

That bitterness dug its claws into my psyche so much that I began to test my faith. I stopped going to church. I stopped believing in anything and everything. It's strange to be mad at a God you are trying not to believe in, but I was angry that my joy was complicated. I wanted carefree joy, and when I didn't experience the entire excitement of my pregnancy – when those fears crept in at night, I tried to protect myself by converting my fears into anger. I was toddler-level angry. I wanted to pout and kick and scream.

That mentality wasn't sustainable. I realized it was up to me to be happy and celebrate the life that was growing inside. Not just the baby growing inside but the new life I was growing into.

I started by believing in myself after I began praying again. I prayed with Dylan for our child and began involving God in my daily life. When I couldn't see a path through the day, I would ask for help getting through the hour. When I couldn't see how to get through the hour, I would ask God for help getting through the minute. Starting to believe in myself felt good, and it led to me having more faith in my baby. I believed he would have the strength to go through what he needed in order to thrive.

I started journaling and reading devotions with a group of women online.

Involving God more in my daily life dissipated my anger and fear. It strengthened my connection with my husband. The walls I placed to protect myself were falling, and instead of isolation, I found community – instead of anxiety, I found hope. I even found a little slice of religion in savoring my cup of coffee and the soft way snow fell on the trees at my house. I thanked God daily for as much good as I could see – even for some of the bad times that gave me a greater understanding of Him. This all led to me feeling better. I felt stronger. It's funny but true how relinquishing control made me feel more in control – how trusting Him for what I could not change gave me the courage to hope.

Struggling with anger is a natural part of any disappointment, but I hope you do not stay with your anger if you are reading this. I hope you find the strength you need, as I did, during whatever trials you face.

I love this quote by Nanea Hoffman, "If today gets difficult, re-member the smell of coffee, the way sunlight bounces off a window, the sound of your favorite person's laugh, the feeling when a song you love comes on, the color of the sky at dusk, and that we are here to take care of each other."

December 9th, 2019

Saturday was another somber day. I couldn't escape my thoughts and didn't leave our bed for most of the morning. I lay on my side, crying next to our dog while looking at the clock on my nightstand as it changed from 10:59 to 11:00 a.m. It wasn't until approximately then that I built enough mental strength to face the day ahead.

You aren't supposed to ask why, but sometimes I can't help it.

Dylan was so helpful and sweet, encouraging me gently to get up. He thought starting on a small project around the house would help occupy my mind.

He admitted he was scared, and we reminded each other that fear is normal and allowed. He also reminded me that we aren't alone because we have each other. I know we are going through this together, but even so, my thoughts went darker and darker today. I was drowning in the unknowns. I felt the full burden of getting our son to at least thirty-nine weeks of pregnancy. Then, I felt the reality that the delivery was just the tip of the medical iceberg we were facing.

Thinking this baby deserves the best possible outcome is what eventually gets me out of bed. I am determined to give it to him however I can.

The Maternal Fetal Medicine we saw specialized in high-risk pregnancies. She was willing to refer me to other mothers like me, who helped answer any questions I had. They are such great people, and I feel blessed to have been introduced to them.

I am also grateful for the Mothers of Omphaloceles page, though today, I didn't have the strength to interact with it. The possibility that our son may not make it to his first breath or may require multiple invasive surgeries, tubes, tests, and more is tough to understand and grasp.

December 9th, 2019

My journey is not a linear one. There are days I feel incredibly grateful to have the gift of a life I value more than my growing inside, and there are days that sink me. I regularly remind myself that there are too many circumstances outside my control. As slow as time feels, I know it's passing quickly, that someday soon, what is unknown will be known, and I will wonder how I ever made it to where I am.

Each day that passes is one day closer to meeting my Omphalocele baby, my sweet "O" warrior. I know Dylan and I will be alongside the next Omphalocele family as they experience the news of this diagnosis and the anxiety and fear.

My hope is often tied to the next step, breath, and decision. My feet don't hit the ground running most days, but being upright is a good start.

"You came into this season not knowing what tomorrow would bring, but you made the brave decision to keep trusting and to keep going, and even on days like this, that means everything."

- Morgan Harper Nichols

CHAPTER 5

The Past Often Informs the Future

I couldn't have guessed the trials of my first pregnancy. I did not know how hard it would be – some days, waking up, standing up, and taking the next breath was like asking me to climb Mount Everest.

Some would think the first trial faced when told your pregnancy is high risk is whether or not to abort. In our situation, it was an option due to his unknown outcome. When I reflect on my decision to proceed with the pregnancy, religious and political affiliations were the last thing on my mind.

The most significant driving force I had was trust. I trusted Dylan to support my decisions. I knew this child was half of him, and I owed it to us both not to give up. From there, I had to trust my body, mind, foundation of faith, and even my unborn son to have the strength to get through.

Being a nurse also helped inform my decision. Knowing about human anatomy and thinking of that tiny heartbeat inside grew the love I had in droves. Medicine and treatments are constantly advancing. I was determined to fight for our son until every option was exhausted and hold on to even the slightest glimmer of hope that we would make it.

My love lit a fire in me. We were growing strong together. I don't mean just me and the baby, but Dylan, too. He supported me and would have no matter what I decided. Our marriage was still new. We couldn't drop our relationship with one another even as we tended to our setbacks.

I started needing him close. Prior to the diagnosis, we were relatively independent. We had separate lives during the day then came together at the end, sometimes only to go to bed beside each other.

I was afraid to be alone, fearing I would miscarry. He reassured me when I expressed concerns about miscarrying. I dreaded his absence – even while he did typical activities like hunting or working late. When I was alone early on, my worries and anxieties consumed me.

It didn't help that the doctors in our area were unfamiliar with Omphaloceles. It is rare in general, but even more so in our rural town.

Because the baby needed a higher level of care like a higher level NICU / Children's Pediatric hospital, I was matched with physicians several hours away for the delivery. I feared the lack of access meant I might not get the care I needed if something went terribly wrong.

I had to trust the doctors, the science, and the medical interventions, but those all fell short of trusting in God. Many people return to God when all other avenues fail, but that thinking is backward. I had to trust God first so I had something substantial to fall back on when all else failed.

I mentioned before that Dylan and I couldn't have known what we would face as a couple – no one gets to see the future. It was the foundation of trust in God, Dylan, and our marriage that I returned to in my darkest moments. Faith sustained us through every bump. The foundation of our past carried us through our present.

December 13th, 2019

We are one month out from our son's initial diagnosis. I got up today and dressed for work. This small act is a BIG deal because I haven't had the energy to invest in myself for a while.

I feel more positive with each passing day. I purchased a cute Boppy nursing pillow cover with cows on it. I love it! I also bought some cow print earrings from a local boutique. The cow print is on the Omphalocele ribbons to commemorate all the babies with it. I have a deeper love for cows and have started to notice them more grazing in the fields at local farms.

It is ironic how the cow was chosen as the print of choice. Many cows are black and white, and I have dealt with more gray areas than ever navigating this pregnancy. The relevance of the cow's colors to me is the balance of dark days that weigh heavy and stop time with lighter days that pass when there is too much to do to focus intently on my fears or days when I am gifted moments of peace. Sometimes, the dark and light coexist on the same day — sometimes in the same moment.

Tonight is my mom's birthday party. I look forward to getting out of the house and out of my head! Tomorrow, we are going to a gluten-free bakery (since I have Celiac Disease) and the Penguins game — more opportunities for distraction.

I spoke with my aunt earlier; she shared her dream with me. In it, my Gram came to her and said, "It will all be okay." I am holding onto that dream and the support from my friends and family.

My next appointment is in eighteen days. I will get additional labs to find more information and make more decisions with those results.

December 13th, 2019

In the meantime, I continue to pray and hope our little bug grows and Dylan and I enjoy more peace as these days pass. I'm so ready to meet our boy. Dylan and I still can't agree on a name.

My excitement grows to be a boy momma. This overwhelming love is beginning to replace my initial fears as the strongest emotion.

I'm so in love already!

I wanted to be a mom as soon as possible after our marriage. Most of our decisions as a married couple were based on that fact.

We chose to stay close to our family and friends, making sure our children felt the support of our parents and extended family while staying in our tight-knit community. We had an immense love for our community and wanted to pass those memories on to our kids and see them create memories with their future families. We also wanted them to grow up in the school system in which my family members and I worked. It was vital for us to have more than one resource to cover the millions of questions that were sure to arise, and staying in our hometown was the perfect solution.

Despite putting these plans into place to thrive within the community where we put our roots down, I often felt isolated during my pregnancy. Dealing with the unexpected almost made me forget the pillars we built to support us. Still, I craved days where I didn't worry as much. I longed for good sleep when many nights found me exhausted, sobbing, and praying through every fear.

When I reminisce on the time before I became pregnant, I am painfully aware of how naive Dylan and I were. We expected our life together to go smoothly, with not even the tiniest bump in the road.

48

My unmet expectations were the source of a barrage of disappointment. We hadn't considered that even normal pregnancies can be difficult. Our excitement to start a family skewed us to the potential for a negative experience. Still, I had to forgive myself for being unaware. These aspects of pregnancy are rarely spoken of, much less taught to the general population.

The perspective I have now granted me the insight to judge what I succeeded in and overcame and areas I could have handled better.

It's a natural reaction to want to know as much information as possible. The amount of data from Google searches and online groups sometimes consumed me. I understand firsthand the false sense of comfort you get from trying to prepare for every outcome.

If I could return to that time, my present self would tell her to breathe – to take one step at a time. I would remind myself not to waste time preparing for what one can never fully prepare. I would remind her to check in emotionally with herself and to check on her husband.

He faced the same trials as me – often alone – and endured the same issues as me, but silently because of the limited resources for men in his position. Looking back, I wish we relied more on each other.

I would also rely more on my family to talk me out of my panic when it rose. I had such an incredible support system, so many relatives all rooting for our little one, and still allowed myself to feel alone.

A close group of work friends helped me through some dark days. I will never forget how they eased my worries just by checking in.

On days I couldn't leave my bed, I reread texts from loved ones, reminding me I wasn't alone.

I wore gifted jewelry to doctor's appointments. A Mother Mary beaded bracelet and an Emerald bangle. Emerald is May's birthstone. It was so precious to wear that reminder of hope that it quickly became my favorite piece of jewelry.

I kept all the ultrasound pictures, and there were many – two hundred plus – each one documentation that he was growing right along with our hopes.

I often spoke directly with our son and tried never to bring up his Omphalocele. I didn't want to define him by that.

December 18th, 2019

I asked Dylan, "Why do you think we have to face this?" His response was, "Because we are strong enough to and will love our son no matter what." I needed that conversation. I needed those words at that exact moment. I couldn't imagine having the peace and confidence he has right now. I admire him for that. It helps calm me. I am sleeping a lot and find it easy to cry.

This pregnancy is the most challenging trial I have ever had to handle. I asked my friends Beta and Carrie from the MOO group how they each handled the unknowns. They both told me it gets easier with time and that leaning on prayer helped them in their hour of need. I have the highest respect for what Beta and Carrie have been through because they shoulder what I am facing now and then use their experiences to encourage me.

I hope to be like them and help other moms in their hour of need as well. I rely on them heavily — sometimes, I fear, too heavily — but they are always gracious when I text them. They respond to our group texts with rapid-fire speed, and it always leads me to cry more in my fears or sigh in relief when a topic I ask about "seems scarier than it is," as they both have lived this very life I am living. I appreciate both sides of it. There is too much at stake for me to be too proud to ask for help. I am grateful for the blessing of their support and hope to get to meet them someday.

The exhaustion of pregnancy hormones, my changing body, and the work of processing my fear about all this devours my energy. I want to sleep until March and wake up when it's time to meet the baby. I remind myself daily of the privilege it is to carry this child.

December 18th, 2019

No matter the outcome, I hold on to that. There are days when I get sad thinking I could miscarry at any time or that our son won't make it. Those are the hardest because I know the best thing for both of us is for me to manage my stress levels. I have to be active in protecting my thoughts from going dark. Each day, I hold on to an idea that gives me strength. Many days, I derive my strength from others. I remind myself of the support I have access to: my doctors, my friends, my family, my community, and especially Dylan. He is my rock, the light part of this dark, the calm to my crazy, and someone who believes in me against all my doubts. He is sweet to me and so good for me. He is trying to stay strong for me, and that gives me the strength to be strong for him too. Life is tough, but loving our baby is the easy part. Our love, both past and present, is the easy part. I know how important that aspect of this pregnancy is. I want our son to look just like Dylan — absolutely gorgeous.

"So it's not gonna be easy. It's gonna be really hard; we're gonna have to work at this every day, but I want to do that because I want you. I want all of you, forever, you and me every day."

– Nicholas Sparks

CHAPTER 6

The Importance of Choosing A Good Life Partner

I rely on the images of mine and Dylan's love when life gets heavy. It sinks me sometimes unexpectedly that we didn't get to float through the pregnancy, enjoying the milestones as other couples did. The fear and the anger always walk beside me, ready to pounce. It's always when I least expect it and rarely at a convenient time when I am tucked away from the world's judging eyes.

We hired Kelsee Forsyth to photograph our wedding. The pictures remind us of a day that was too surreal to remember accurately in the moment we lived it. I would almost suggest a photographer to capture the other moments – the private ones. Who knows if we should show the world or keep it to ourselves, but shouldn't our fears be held along with our triumphs? Surely, there are others out there who need to see someone else falling apart when facing the same circumstances. Surviving is its own triumph in times like these.

In discussing what it was like to process a high-risk diagnosis, I barely scratched the surface of what it was like just to be pregnant. Between the start of the pregnancy and the diagnosis, I rapidly dropped weight, and I couldn't keep any food down. In total, I lost seventeen pounds. Even fresh air made me dry-heave. I had a constant headache and only craved spicy food. I barely slept. To say I was accosted on all fronts, physical, mental, and spiritual, was an understatement.

My external mood was stable during this time. Internally, however, pregnancy rewires you into someone unrecognizable. There are concerns I never would have considered that made an unhappy home in my mind. I caught myself balancing the relief that our wish had come true with the feeling that our relationship may have benefited from more time spent with just the two of us.

In all of this, I was less bothered by the worries I had prior to becoming pregnant. Change can add worries, but it can also replace them. Overall, I mastered control of what was controllable and grew exponentially by allowing myself grace over what I could not control, despite the hold OCD often has on me.

In the column labeled Things you can't control, at the top was the fact that "high-risk pregnancy" would now be riddled throughout my medical chart, and there was no hope of any future pregnancy escaping that label.

I'm now going to dive into what's less comfortable and least talked about – being intimate with my husband. Mom and Dad, you can skip over this section!

About halfway through the second trimester, Dylan and I stopped being intimate. In my head, I feared it would hurt the baby or cause a miscarriage. I know now that in most pregnancies, sex shouldn't hurt the fetus, but later, my OBGYN explained that due to the high-risk nature and not wanting preterm labor to occur, we could abstain. Prior to the self-inflicted celibacy, I had minor cramping after sex and occasionally bleeding. It caused me to fear that I would start bleeding heavily and lose the baby. I knew if there was any reason we lost him, I didn't want it to be something that I could have played a role in preventing.

I inadvertently set up a huge physical block towards Dylan and sometimes a mental one, too. He didn't deserve to be placed on the back burner, but I admit that sometimes, my fears got the best of me. The other aspect that I was not warned about is how much energy it takes to create life. It left me with crumbs to give at the end of each day. It consumed so much of my time, energy, love, and mental energy that little was left over to give to anyone else.

Dylan and I both knew it was not a vindictive decision but a necessary one. Still, I wanted to connect with him. I wanted to be desired and even pursued. That doesn't disappear. Subconsciously, I put up a wall that created a void in our relationship. It's so important to me that I share this aspect of our relationship because no one warned us. It wasn't something we prepared for or anticipated. It took us months to rebuild that part of our relationship after the birth. I wish it had gone differently.

The doctors suggested pelvic rest to prevent early preterm contractions, which meant no sex. The inability to connect outside of sex threatened both Dylan and me with a new level of isolation. I learned that it's easiest to block out the people that mean the most to us. Still, it made us creative with the ways we showed affection to one another. We cuddled on the couch, talked to each other, cried together, and showered together.

54

At night, we lay down in bed and read to the baby together. This habit became a personal favorite way for us to connect during this time.

There are so many opportunities to connect with your spouse. The lack of physical connection is temporary. I encourage you to find new ways to connect to your spouse without waiting for the circumstances to throw you into it. There are many journeys to spousal love, all beautiful, relevant, and worthy of our efforts.

Desiring physical intimacy with our spouse is a natural part of being attracted to them. It's a different kind of closeness. The best part about intimacy is that it can grow even after long periods of being stagnant. It takes effort from both people in the partnership, but the outcome is worth it.

I learned that intimacy can even improve when your body changes. A woman's body is fantastic. You don't have to love the stretch marks and extra skin, but neither should you fixate or reject them. They are the reminders of your child's first home – their first safe place. They remind Dylan and me of what we walked through together – imperfectly, but together.

"It's okay to feel alone, lost, and empty. For everything that's lonely, it finds its company, everything lost is meant to be found, and everything empty eventually gets filled. So, see it like this: Think of all the terrible times you have lived through. Think about how they, too, have passed. You're a survivor, and you have to go through hell to find heaven. The same way you must break in order to find yourself again."

- R. M. Drake

CHAPTER 7

Some Woowoo to Get Me Through

It may seem woo-woo or out there, but I speak from my lived experiences. My Grandma Edna passed away before we became pregnant, but I am convinced it was her guidance that gave me my initial feelings that something was not right with the pregnancy from the start. I wasn't left in my doubts even as my fears turned into reality.

I have this image of Dylan's Nan and my grandma sitting on a porch somewhere in Heaven, talking about us. They used to work together in a local hospital and became fairly close. They saw less of each other as time went on, but I am certain they enjoyed watching their family expand as new generations were born. I consider them our guardian angels.

While our grandmas weren't earthbound, I recognized other living, breathing godsends. They came in the form of our medical team. From our ultrasound techs and other medical professionals to our OBGYN and our maternal-fetal medicine doctor, we could not have been better surrounded.

I still talk to my Grandma Edna, thanking her for being here still and for sending me so many living angels as well as the signs.

December 23rd, 2019

We celebrated Christmas early as a family with my parents and sister. It was lovely, as usual. I had such a nice time. Evelyn, my niece, is adorable. I caught myself fixated on her movement. I'm so fascinated by the miracle she is — the miracle we all are, really.

Recently, she developed the ability to hold her bottle. I love her big, beautiful eyes, how they look like they want to soak in all the newness of this world she is discovering. This is her first Christmas. My parents gifted her a hand-painted stool and a children's book that matched. The stool was beautifully detailed, and it made me hope our son would have one of his own someday. I am overwhelmed with sadness when I consider he may not have a first Christmas, the opportunity to receive a thoughtful gift or to feel how much love can fit into a room.

I am disappointed that not even Christmas can keep the fears at bay.

In the truck on the way home, I admitted those thoughts to Dylan. He asked me to explain why we couldn't have our son at Christmas this year. I began crying, and once they fell, the tears wouldn't stop. I was ugly crying, my whole body shaking in sobs. I kept everything inside for too long at that point. My smiles became more and more fake as the day went on. I cried the rest of the day - more tears than I thought a human could produce. I needed to release that. Dylan understands. He held my hand and promised me he'd get me one of those stools. Both of us knew it wasn't about the stool, but through my tears, I told him I wanted one with the Lorax painted on it.

I haven't thought this much about anxiety and depression as much as I did during that holiday season. I have been aware of them for most of my life, but never the way they presented in those weeks.

December 23rd, 2019

It felt good to cry that day in the truck on the way home, but I knew I was more lost than I had ever been before. I never wanted to be on any medication — not even antibiotics, but I had to cave. I made an appointment with the doctor to explain how sick I was. I was prescribed Keflex twice a day and put on an inhaler. During that time, I was trying my hardest to heal, but I went six weeks of not breathing well, and it finally caught up with me. My chest was on fire, and it was a constant struggle to get adequate air to my lungs. I was sleeping nightly in a recliner to ease the shortness of breath.

It can only get better from here. My job now is to rest, heal, and love this baby with all I have by taking care of myself. I hope my spirits improve for Christmas Day.

This morning, Dylan kissed me and then leaned over to kiss my stomach. I loved it so much. I'm grateful that it's him. It's always been him.

I walked bags of change to my car this morning and tripped with some falling out. Sure enough, I found a heads-up penny outside my car door. Again, I know it may be a little woo-woo for some, but for me and my grandma, I know what it really means. It means everything will work out even if I can't see it yet. It means no matter what, I will win in the end. We will win in the end. I am counting every lucky star, and every blessing, and holding fast to every heads-up penny until my baby is safe in my arms.

"It is worth remembering that the time of greatest gain in terms of wisdom and inner strength is often that of greatest difficulty."

- Dalai Lama XIV

CHAPTER 8

"So, you come here often?"

My fondest memory of our wedding day happened at the nacho bar at our reception. Dylan slid beside me and said, "So, do you come here often?" He had the simplest ways of putting a smile on my face. He was always the cheesy one (pun intended).

Say what you will about the institution of marriage. Still, when I stood before my husband and our family, I was also standing on the promise I made to be his partner – to face whatever came as a team to grow together with intentionality. He made the same promise. When the time came for him to act on his commitment, he did. I used his shoulder as a snot rag, an untold amount. I filled his ears with every last fear I had at all hours of the day and night. He was never "off," never too busy, and returned every concern of mine into reassurance. His strength was the beacon I turned to and walked toward when I couldn't find my own. It didn't just hold me up; it made me stronger and more able to hold myself. Together, we were fighting for a solution instead of fighting with each other. That's an important distinction. We knew the stakes and what we fought for. It was our child. There were so many heavy moments, but Dylan provided pockets of levity just by being his tender and humorous self. Without him, I may not have laughed that entire nine months. As the pregnancy moved along and we got more comfortable with the unknowns, I started to resolve that I wanted to help others facing similar issues.

That's when I learned about Grady's Decision.

Grady's Decision is a local organization that began after a couple lost their son in the Neonatal Intensive Care Unit – NICU. His twin sister survived. In the process of their grief, the family that started Grady's Decision wanted to honor their son's memory by helping others. Their organization offers support, prayer, and financial assistance to families of children in the NICU. They provide gas cards, food vouchers, and parking fees to people with children in the hospital. Dylan and I were referred to them by one of my best friends Kaitlyn when they anticipated we would be staying in the NICU after our son was born.

They came to our aid well before delivery, and I was able to speak with my sponsor numerous times prior to our delivery to prepare.

My sponsor, Amy, was the aunt of the twins. She was the main driver of the help and connections formed during the last five weeks of my pregnancy. I spoke over the phone with her. I could tell by the grace and reassurance she gave me that her faith was strong. We refer to ourselves as a Grady family and our son as a Grady baby. Because of our connections to this organization, we had an outpouring of prayer and support through his birth. We remain friends with many of them.

I planned to join the Love Team, a group of people who support and help families just like ours. I am grateful we were aware of the NICU stay, but not every family is. This journey drove me to want to help as many people as I could to make sure they never felt alone in the NICU. The kind of sacrificial love we received from Grady's Decision was a force that drove me to want to give back.

If you want to read the full story behind Grady's Decision, their website is www.gradysdecision.com. I recommend giving it a read and supporting them if you are able.

January 3rd, 2020

Christmas was a great day. However, I felt my thoughts rob me of joy that day. My thoughts overwhelmed me with question after unanswered questions. I had several significant appointments scheduled on New Year's Eve, and the worry of whether those would present new questions or invite new fears led me to be less than one hundred percent in the moment.

On New Year's Eve, I was scheduled for a fetal echocardiogram and routine ultrasound. The first exam was to check the structure of our son's heart. Dylan and I decided to take our mothers with us to spend some quality time with them so they would have a chance to experience the baby's movements captured on a large screen.

I was incredibly nervous about the test showing an abnormality in the heart, so I talked the entire car drive to prevent my fears from making it to the front of my consciousness.

I almost went into a panic attack, lying on the table for the fetal echo. Dylan, my mom, and my mother-in-law were there by my side. They were able to see his face in 4D on the screen. There wasn't a dry eye in the room. Our mothers were astonished at the way technology improved since they were pregnant! We got the news that his heart was perfect and clear. We did not have to follow up for any cardiology workups until birth. It was the news I prayed for — news I so desperately needed. I bawled when they told me he beat the odds associated with Omphaloceles. Forty percent of these babies have cardiac issues. This appointment was the first that ended in a win for us! We wouldn't need a cardiac team for delivery. I was glad to cross off one of the worries on my never-ending list. My heart needed that. The ultrasound was next.

January 3rd, 2020

They were working the paddle against my stomach for a long time. There was suspicion of dilated bowels. Dilated bowels can mean a lot of things, but the biggest concern was that they would rupture or perforate. If they ruptured, the contents of his colon would explode into his abdomen, making him very ill or likely end his life. If they were perforated, it meant the hole would be smaller, but to the same effect, eventually rendering that part of his intestines incapable of doing its job. I was relieved when the doctor entered the room to repeat the scan herself and ruled this concern out. His growth was good at that appointment, but we knew that could change at any time. It was always in the back of my mind.

For now, I will breathe and trust God the way I have up until this point. Dr. Christina is transferring to the Women's Hospital in Pittsburgh. I am sad she is leaving us in DuBois, but I am looking forward to following up with her there if our paths align. Many aspects of this pregnancy are about waiting, holding our breath at each test, sighing with the good news, praying at the setbacks, and the cycle continues. For now, I'm trusting my maternal instincts; they rarely steer me wrong.

I have never been so excited to lay my eyes on someone like this precious little boy in my entire life. I am looking forward to meeting another Omphalocele baby and her family this weekend from a few towns over. It will be lovely to meet in person and to witness the miracle and survival of another child like ours. I am continuing to pray that we make it to full term between thirty-eight and thirty-nine weeks. This finish line of sorts gives him the best chance of having the strength to survive. The word miracle continues to pop into my head. Miracle, miracle, miracle: It's nothing short of a miracle to be carrying a new generation. We are drenched in them.

"I love people who have been through adversity and heartache and obstacles as impossible as the sun itself. They usually make it out with hearts as warm as gold. Cores made of fire. Lives soaked with full intention. Hope like another morning. They know how to start again, how to walk through walls with palms wide open, and how to begin at the edge and end. Those, to me, are the best people."

– Victoria Erickson

CHAPTER 9

Get By With a Little Help From My Friends

Allow me a minute to stand on a podium like I just won a Grammy. Imagine my dress flowing to the floor, the auditorium lights creating a satin shine that runs the length. As I get to the podium, I pull out the list of all the people that got me to this point in my life. I'd thank God, my husband, mother, and sisters first, and my friends – but that list would take much longer.

My friends' support came at the perfect time. It was given unhindered without condition or reciprocation, and that is the reason I made it. It's challenging to say the words, "I made it," because the truth is we made it. Each person tied their success with mine and fought like hell to make it happen. They were the support beams of a bridge that I couldn't possibly cross alone. To each and every one of my friends, thank you.

My friendship with Meagan started with a Facebook message I pre-typed the night before the ultrasound appointment when we received our son's diagnosis. In the message, I told her I had a strange intuition that something was wrong. I couldn't figure out why I felt so sure of it. Meagan was caring for her own son at the time, who had a congenital heart defect that was unknown until the day of birth. I felt she would have a unique understanding of our plight. Just in case I was completely wrong about my gut instincts, I waited until the next day. In the midst of the shock I felt learning of our son's omphalocele, I sent the message to Meagan. Her compassion and support for us was swift. Her courage to face what she was going through was a testament to the love she had for her son. She gave me a great example of what it looks like to gift yourself grace, and she showed me how to grant myself the grace it takes to endure. She was a walking example I could rely on for strength amidst the many storms I faced. I am forever thankful for the bond we formed over our similar experiences.

Beta and Carrie were more local to me and allowed me an intimate look into their journeys. Both of their children had Omphaloceles. As sad as it was to connect over these dire circumstances, it felt like there was more help draining the water out of a sinking ship.

Alyssa and Kingslea both lived states away. I met them on the Mothers of Omphalocele page. Kingslea was my go-to girl who was pregnant with an Omphalocele baby girl and had a due date just a few days before mine. Alyssa had a son who was already defying the odds as he was living with his Omphalocele. Their journey was one I prayed for ours to mimic. Our kids faced various hardships both in and out of the womb, but the silver lining of it all was how strong we all became together. Often, friendships have a natural conclusion.

Circumstantial friendships tend to fade when life changes. The new house you move to a couple of towns away, a new job that decreases the time you have to spend with them, or new relationship, another baby, or an ailing parent – there are many reasons why friendships fizzle out. There's something different – most lasting in friendships that are born from adversity, a shared struggle. We became stronger because of each other.

January 6th, 2020

It's another Monday. The new week has me checking off my pregnancy countdown. I almost made it to twenty-one weeks.

I am unsure why I give an audience to every possible fear. Our son may need a tracheotomy. He may have Beckwith-Wiedemann syndrome and may need oxygen to support his lungs. The concerns are valid. It's a lot to face. I ask God to show me examples of good outcomes so that I have a beacon to show me the way to hope. If I consider it, I think He has already done so. The new friends I made in the Omphalocele community, the caring medical team assigned to our care, our son's growth in the past two months, and even the little kicks in my stomach I'm beginning to feel. I hold onto these signs. I'm halfway through the start of this ordeal.

Dylan always said we are the lucky ones. I remind myself how we are not among the one in every four females who struggle with fertility. Although we came close to the end of one year trying without success, we did conceive this baby. We have the gift of this new life to foster, nurture, and grow. The duality of life is that it's all so fragile, but each one of us has within us the capability to be brave and strong. There's a strong desire to go on no matter what odds we face.

We met with a local Omphalocele family, and they are truly amazing. The feeling of community and companionship we are finding is not lost on me. We were alone when this all began. We were facing the specifics of medically complex pregnancy blindly until we found that support. It makes me feel good to know them and cheer on their successes. Their daughter is a source of light for me. When I feel down, I recall some of the sweet moments we had with her.

January 6th, 2020

Dylan got to meet with a father who had gone through this ordeal. I'm glad he had a chance to talk to this dad because I know there are anxieties and helplessness associated with dads who have to watch their spouses go through this. I am grateful to be a part of their story. They are giving back to us, which feels exceptionally generous given all they have been through.

When we met at the restaurant, I was somewhat afraid to see their daughter. I'm not sure exactly what I pictured I would see, but the first time I saw her, she looked perfect and healthy. That moment shifted my perspective on this pregnancy, and I felt the beginning threads of hope. For the first time, I was not shutting it out. I am allowing myself to hope that this will be okay.

The next goal is to make it to my next appointment in three weeks without any issues. Time flies, and my anxiety still finds ways to check in on me. A priest is coming to bless our house tomorrow. I'll do anything to give us the best chance for a favorable outcome! I picked up a mandarin orange from the fruit bowl and saw it had a little bump on the side that looked just like an Omphalocele. I thought to myself how that orange, even with its bump, is still very much an orange. Similarly, our son, even with this birth defect, is very much just like other babies. I snapped a picture of it. I don't want to forget any sign, big or small, that we can do this.

"You never know how hard someone had it before they became soft, and you never know the ugliness they had to go through to have such a beautiful heart. Sometimes, we learn grace from the worst times of our lives, and that's what saves us."

- Stephanie Bennett Henry

CHAPTER 10

A Diagnosis Away from a Different Life

The day of our son's echo test, I wore special bracelets. One had a heart charm; another featured Mother Mary and the last had a charm that said: "Stronger Than The Storm." I thought of how I found a few pennies heads up along the way so far, and I held onto hope that luck was on our side today.

"Your son's echo was normal," the doctor said.

Did that mean we could let down our guard?

The doctor explained our son *may* still have a heart issue at birth, but it would be difficult to diagnose a minor cardiac issue in utero due to imaging difficulties. So with that, I wondered if we could float through this possible phase of normalcy – and how long this feeling would last. I had to walk through several wards of the hospital in Pittsburgh, passing person after person, each waiting to see the results of themselves or those they love. Each person there was one diagnosis away from a different life. I wondered how many of them had to say goodbye to loved ones sooner than they wanted. Maybe I thought that way to avoid thinking about my situation. I often felt one medical obstacle away from an entire breakdown.

The echo scan took so long that I was sure it was going to be another one of those *bad news* days. When the doctor shared that the echo was normal, my heart dropped out of my throat, and I was able to take a huge breath that I felt myself holding up until that point. By this time, I had multiple family members and friends praying day and night over our son. This win felt personal. Our prayers were working.

Do you know the volunteers who hand out cups of water or Gatorade during long races? The relief felt like that. The road was long ahead of us, but we had people cheering for us along the way. I fully anticipated the worst news but kept suppressing my tears and anxious thoughts. When the doctor told me his heart was clear, I couldn't hold back anymore. I cried so much in that office. I remember telling the doctor and ultrasound

73

technician, who had the most concerned look on their faces, that these were happy tears and how glad I was for the positive news.

"I've never been more relieved to hear the word *normal*," I told them. When I heard the words spoken out loud, it stung. All I wanted was a *normal* pregnancy, and I found myself still mourning the loss of one.

I was grateful that my family was able to be next to me during that significant appointment. They got to celebrate the win with us. Had there been any different outcome, I would have gotten a list of questions answered and moved on from that. For the time being, there were no more questions to ask. The fact that this all happened on New Year's Eve and that good news bookmarked the end of a tumultuous few months made it that much better. I got a glimpse of restored hope just in time for a new year.

January 8th, 2020

The baby's heartbeat was 145 at our appointment yesterday. The OBGYNs are trying their best to keep everyone positive but prepared.

A priest came to bless our house. It was the first time we did something like that. We walked through the house with him. When we got to the nursery, I was excited and thankful that he was willing to bless it for us. It was all so fascinating to me. As the priest went from room to room, blessing each one, we chatted. He reminded me to focus on what was ahead but not to get caught up in things that were too far ahead.

Preparation is essential, but dwelling on variables that we can't predict doesn't help us. He reminded us of what we had at that moment. Dylan and I had each other, our son, and the hope for all this could be.

Right after the priest left, I felt two large kicks on the outside of my belly this time. Dylan felt two more. It could have been a coincidence or another good sign from Heaven — whatever it was, I needed it. The kicks were a new way to connect with the life inside. It was perfect. I am holding on tighter to the simple pleasures of life. I saw a girl I graduated from high school with and her two beautiful kids. Seeing them thrive no longer sends me into a week-long date with my bed.

It makes me excited to see our son's perfect face and even his imperfect belly. My resolve is growing by the day. I'm still not into maternity clothes. The combination of the stress and nausea led me to lose just shy of twenty pounds, but I'm finally back to my starting weight. This will help build up my strength for delivery and is helpful for our son, too. I am feeling strong and got the flu shot to pass on some antibodies to our little guy.

January 8th, 2020

It was nice to see the face of my OBGYN this week with a clear eye unstained by the constant stream of tears. I already know I'll never be the same girl she hugged in my office after I found out our baby had an Omphalocele. I've changed so much since I saw those two pink lines last August. I like who I am becoming — who we are becoming together.

January 10th, 2020

I keep waking up with the worst headaches. I assume this is from stress. The journey seems to drag at times, but here we are at twenty-one weeks. The magnitude of concerns we face is unwavering. Still, the presence of God dwells closely. This week, I felt a peace I hadn't been able to grasp for a long time. It is surprising to have the space to hold peace and fear at the same time. The fear doesn't get the best of the peace anymore like it used to.

I'm feeling all the kicks now. Feeling him every day is like having my confirmation that he's there, wanting to meet me as much as I meet him. Milkshakes make him move more, so I'll have to keep drinking them.

I logged into my patient portal to check on my upcoming appointments. I noticed we were pre-scheduled to see both the genetic doctor and the surgeon assigned to us on the same day. I already feel emotional about both of those visits. What better way to handle it than to just get it done in the same day? I checked in on the Mothers of Omphalocele page and saw that one of the mothers miscarried. There hasn't been much good news lately on it, but I can't stop checking in. I care greatly about these people and their stories.

January 10th, 2020

My heart sank to learn of her loss. I cried over that page more than anything lately and shared that story with a coworker. I sleep more now. I know it is good for me and essential for my health, but at times, I'm using it as an escape. I looked down at my stomach today, and even though I'm measuring about four weeks behind in size, my pants feel tighter. It may be time to start looking for maternity clothes. I'm going to see if the ones my friend let me borrow fit first, then check the Goodwill if not. I was thinking this morning how tragic and unfair it is that you can lose a baby at any point during your pregnancy, but that's the same with anyone in your life. Our situation offers a unique perspective on life. When you become acquainted with mortality — take daily walks with the unknown — there is a stark clarity of what is most important. I have transformed the way I love people since this all happened. I love more intentionally. Before this, I didn't want to overdo affection towards anyone. I held back. Now, I instead steer my intentions to avoid underselling my love for someone. My hugs last longer, my tears flow more freely, and I take my time with every goodbye. I've been reflecting lately on how much worse this could have been instead of my previous mindset that gave an audience to every fear. Seventeen more days until we see his face again. I am so grateful for ultrasounds.

"Grace is the face that love wears
when it meets imperfection.."

- Joseph R. Cooke

CHAPTER 11

Managing Grief

One of the many aspects of having a medically complex pregnancy is the way you walk with grief. It's a different grief than those who experience a pregnancy loss feel, but it's just as valid. Processing grief isn't linear. You can't rationalize your way out of it. That was one of the hardest parts for me – that and the fact that grief has many levels. There's nuance and complexity to it. It's because we can love something or someone so much that makes loss feel so strong. I was mourning the loss of a "normal" pregnancy. Up until my pregnancy, I did not consider myself prone to self-pity. But while riding the wave of this journey, there were days I could milk five minutes of feeling sorry for myself into a three-day doom spiral. I didn't know why it felt so good to indulge in feelings of self-pity. It took considerable effort and community support to rescue me from the places where grief had swallowed me. Every time I put down a layer of suffering and replaced it with hope, it revealed a new strength I didn't realize I had. This pattern revealed itself as grace. The opposite of self-pity is self-grace. It's okay to feel the full effect of what weighs on you. Having grace for those feelings, giving them time to pass, being honest with yourself about where you are at, and asking for help are all ways that grace can save you from being consumed by self-pity.

January 13th, 2020

Another new week begins — another Monday. I am starting to feel pregnant each time our little man moves. Saturday, I thought about my planned C-Section and got more and more upset that our son was going to be cut out of me.

It threw me into a complete panic attack, and it took a long time for me to get my heart rate under control. Afterwards, all I wanted to do was sleep. Dylan was aware of my anxiety and did his best to reassure me. I've been reminding myself how our son is safer inside me now than he would be out in this world. If he is content there, warm, and loved, then I need to be as well.

My best friend Kaitlyn is pregnant as well. We are both going through it in our own ways! Her pregnancy is not complex, but she still helps me stay sane. We remind each other of what we do have. It helps immensely to have someone to go to who can take you from the complex web of fear to remembering the most basic ways you are loved and cling to those. I hope we can always be there for each other.

In two short weeks, I'll get to see our son's face again. My sister Chelcee is helping pick out a crib with our parents and bringing my vision for the nursery to life. I can already tell the next three months will fly by, and there's more work to do in preparation for his arrival. I decided the theme for his nursery should be adventure, with mountains, peaks, and valleys. How fitting.

After explaining to my sister what I imagined the nursery to look like, a what-if thought intruded. What if we never have a baby to fill this room? What if I never bring our son to this home? We decided that if it came to that, we would donate everything.

January 13th, 2020

Even if I get pregnant sometime in the future, the visual reminders would be too difficult to keep around. Some family members keep trying to convince me to have a baby shower. I can't bring myself to have one. It's not fair to Dylan and me to have a room full of baby items we may not get to use. Also, having a baby shower is like telling the universe we have hope. Having hope feels scary. It gives us something to hold onto that can be taken away — more than that, it could be completely demolished.

 Dylan got a job offer on Saturday and is considering it. We both understand that change may be the last thing we need right now, but I want him to take it. He is so deserving of it. Honestly, he is one of the hardest-working people I know. Our concern with a new job is his ability to have paid time off if our son is hospitalized for an extended period or if I need more assistance after the delivery. Because of his medical needs, we already know our son will be in the NICU. It's a question of how long that stay will be. I encouraged Dylan to ask his potential employers about the specifics of how much time he was allowed. I reminded him that whatever his decision was, I wanted to be here to support him fully in it. I think he owes it to himself to explore this new option despite all the changes ahead. What's one more?

 Later on that night, I was organizing the few items we had in the nursery and started to cry. I know now never to do that task alone again. I thought I was strong enough to tackle the job, but I was not. I wouldn't wish the feeling of hopelessness on anyone. Simple tasks become that much harder when every bit of joy is wrapped up in the possibility that it could be taken away.

January 13th, 2020

Still, even as I sat there, I heard a voice in my head that sounded like my own. It said, "You are brave, even in your weakest moments. You got this!" Dylan interrupted my sadness as he came in to check on me (was I crying that loudly?) and just held me. He is so practiced in this form of patience. He never withholds his care, but he did suggest I not attempt these soul-crushing tasks on my own.

He's not wrong.

January 15th, 2020

A quote I saw from a mother on the Omphalocele support page shook me to my core. She said, "He made me strong — as if he changed my DNA." For every day I was in emotional turmoil, there seemed to be a parallel day where my strength surprised me. I'm learning that in life, we meet many versions of ourselves. I am learning about this new version of myself as I go. Each time I thought I couldn't go to another appointment or face another day of stress, I did. I do go on and face whatever comes that day. I am holding the duality of this difficulty while cherishing the thought of being a mother.

I am leaning into my faith now and praying daily. I have also been making every attempt to get to the gym. It's painful most days, but I'm trying to show up the best I can. Some days, all I have in me is to take a walk with my aunt. I will need to get more maternity clothes soon. Nothing fits me. I'm at twenty-two weeks and finally starting to notice my stomach looks pregnant. I consider that an accomplishment.

January 15th, 2020

I am convinced I'm carrying the carbon copy of my husband. Most moms joke about how they have to carry the bulk of the struggle to have their child look like its father. I'm excited to see Dylan 2.0.

January 17th, 2020

One of my biggest crutches during this pregnancy is music. I've been blasting "What It's Like" by Everlast3. The song reminds me that everyone faces hardships. Someone who looks perfectly normal could be going through the most challenging trial of their life. I also relate to the song because explanations would fall short of helping people understand what we are going through. It's the type of situation you need to experience to understand it in its fullness. I enjoy the part of the song that says, "I've seen the good side of bad and the downside of up and everything in between." Best. Line. Ever. We all have days that have us questioning what could happen next. Music has been a passion of mine since I got my first iPod back in middle school. I felt so tough and hyped, jamming to hip-hop and rap before soccer games. I listened to music while studying for my NCLEX nursing exam. I need background noise to get me through the day.

Lately, I have been listening to and relating to music that has never piqued my interest before. I enjoy connecting to songs that wouldn't have spoken to me in another circumstance. Another song that got me through so many dark times is "Look Up Child" by Lauren Daigle. Christian music was never my thing, but I found so much hope in that song. I sing it in my car at the top of my lungs. I'm not the best singer, but I don't care.

January 17th, 2020

There is so much power when she sings,

> You're not threatened by the war.
>
> You're not shaken by the storm.
>
> I know you're in control.
>
> Even in our suffering,
>
> even when it can't be seen,
>
> I know you're in control.4

The baby is kicking me hard these days. I get so happy every time. Dylan has been there to feel more of them. Last night, in the shower, it hit me how much more positive the last few days have been. I am encouraging myself as a form of self-care. I am proud of my growth lately. It's funny that when we were not getting pregnant, I said, "By January, if I'm not pregnant, I'm going back to school to pursue my RN degree." Now, it's January, and I'm twenty-two weeks pregnant, and what a ride it's been so far. How lucky I am to have my boys. They made me strong, as if they changed my DNA.

January 21st, 2020

Last night, I found out a cousin of ours is pregnant. I didn't expect it to overwhelm me like it did. I was hoping to be the only pregnant person because of the complexities of it. I wanted to limit the comparisons of our pregnancies and lessen my constant comparisons of how I wish our pregnancy were versus the reality of how it is. I am excited for everyone I know who is pregnant, but I can't help but also feel sad about our situation. I feel selfish for even writing that. Then I get upset at myself for feeling the envy I do.

January 21st, 2020

I keep reminding myself we have him — our son. We have him, no matter the outcome. Dylan and I are parents. Nothing can change that. I cried a lot over this.

I think winter is making life more difficult, too. I have less fresh air and long walks. I can't keep my windows open because it's too cold. The sun only seems to shine four hours per day.

I asked for an extra ultrasound because I couldn't wait. It was feeding my anxieties. In the meantime, I've been leaning on my mom. We cry together some days. I wish I didn't have to rely so heavily on her. Strangely, I feel guilty, like I'm bothering her or taking up her time, needing her so much. I never want to cause her any hardship, and as my mom, she hurts for this, too. I realize I haven't asked her how she feels, but I am starting to grasp how much a mother can care for her child.

I am learning more about myself now more than ever. I'm permitting myself to cry when I need to and see that as a sign of my strength rather than a weakness. I feel brave for choosing to persevere and allow the pregnancy to progress naturally. It hasn't been easy taking the "wait and see" approach, but I am comforted that I am giving him a chance.

This type of love is different from any other I felt before. When you are a child, you love your parents, but it's a receiving love — one born of necessity. Later, you fall in love with your romantic partner. This type of love is reciprocal — you both contribute to its growth and nurture it. This love, however, is above the rest. It is the other side of a bridge you cross, never to return. Nothing can take it away, and you will never be the same person after experiencing it.

"Sometimes, you get what you want.
Other times, you get a lesson in
patience, timing, alignment, empathy,
compassion, faith, perseverance,
resilience, humility, trust, meaning,
awareness, resistance, purpose, clarity,
grief, beauty, and life. Either way,
you win."

- Brianna Wiest

CHAPTER 12

Hope Kicks

January 24th, 2020

Everyone at work knows I am pregnant, and a handful of people I trust know the full situation. I can't conceal my pregnant belly much longer. I'm not even sure if I'm hiding it well or if I care that anyone knows. I shared the news with the last of the people who were probably too polite to ask and received lots of hugs today. Everyone is excited and happy for me. I still feel calm as long as Dylan is close. I am at ease with my family and friends as well.

Tonight I'm shopping with my friends Nicole M. and Lauren. I always have the best time with them. It gives me a chance to forget about my worries and be human for a little while. I often forget I am carrying around such a heavy situation when I am with them. Those two women and my other friend, Wendy, have been incredible blessings to me. Their support during the hard times, as well as the good, means the world to me and then some.

The days seem to be flying by now. When I have a chance to reflect, I can hardly believe I'm almost twenty-four weeks along. I wish I could share more about the specifics of what's going on with the teachers I work with, but those who do know have been supportive and helpful.

I had some emotional setbacks this week, but I am remaining steadfast.

I got earrings for the local Omphalocele moms I befriended and sent them in the mail. I hope they arrive before the thirty-first, which is National Omphalocele Awareness Day. I am glad they have a day to celebrate and recognize the condition. I'm hoping to be able to celebrate it as a milestone with our son next year.

January 24th, 2020

I want our son to never doubt how incredible it is to us that he continues to thrive. I know he has an uncertain road ahead, and we plan on being there for every hurdle. I am confident of this because I see it with my own eyes in the other families we met going through this. Today, I feel blessed to have made it this far along without any more issues. We continue to put the power of prayer to the test, and it continues to surprise us joyfully.

January 27th, 2020

Today, we have another appointment. I have mixed feelings every time — grateful to see our son's face and terrified they will find something else wrong. Each time, I hold my breath, fake a smile, and pretend to have a positive outlook. I'm seeing a new doctor who wants to assess me because of my high-risk pregnancy. Every change sends me into a dread spiral. I keep reminding myself that his job is to grow, my job is to continue to carry him and nurture him the best way I know how, and the rest will work itself out. I'm doing my best to eat high-quality, nutritious meals despite having Celiac disease. So far, he has been just fine in there. It's a mind versus body game. I barely know who will win: I keep playing the game. I refuse to curl into a ball and cry all day. He needs me strong, so I'll fake it if I have to. I am strong for him.

I pray harder on appointment days that no more organs work their way into his Omphalocele. I also pray he is in the best position to get the full anatomy scan. This is the only way for us to keep track of his progress.

January 27th, 2020

I am looking forward to seeing our favorite ultrasound tech today. It feels like a friendship formed between us. She is the sweetest.

I remind myself multiple times per day that the outcome is up to God and try to surrender it all to Him. Dylan and I have done all we can do to control it, but only God has total control over this. I also remind myself to focus on the strength within myself more than on my shortcomings. I'm processing a slew of worries that won't let me go, and I want to write a list so I can divide it into what I can and can't control.

1. Our son's growth slows or stops.
2. The fluid in his chest wall (ascites) grows, causing him to go into cardiac arrest.
3. That he gets to hear my voice tell him I love him — even better if he has an understanding of what that means.
4. Dilated bowels may cause bowel obstructions.
5. His stomach or another organ moves into his Omphalocele.
6. His organs need to stay aligned and not become rotated.

In my mind, this feels no less than a thousand worries, but as I see the list of six concerns, it makes the fear more manageable.

Maybe this new doctor will have good news. My grief is wrapped up in all the love I have for our son. There is beauty in that. Every concern and unknown circumstance will reveal itself in time. Patience, patience, patience, I keep repeating to myself. Patience is what keeps each day moving forward. It's an uncomfortable friend that I'm learning to rely on.

January 27th, 2020

I am breathing through it all and trying to get into a better mind frame before the appointment. I've done all I can to prepare and will report back when I get the results of the scan.

January 29th, 2020

The results showed good growth. Our little peanut moved into the 50th percentile, weighing approximately 1 pound, 7 ounces. Most Omphalocele pregnancies don't even show up in the percentile chart, so we are doubly relieved. They couldn't find his bladder today, but Mary and Nicole, my nurse and ultrasound tech, reassured me that this probably is because it's empty.

We also found out that some of his intestines may be inside the Omphalocele. That news was less worrisome to me than I thought it would be. From now through delivery, we will keep a close eye on the sac because organs can still move around freely in there. He looks so good to me like he's strong and wants to tell us he's still in the fight. His kicks are stronger every day. I'm starting to feel pressure in my pelvis.

The new Maternal Fetal Medicine doctor in town seems brilliant. He seems to have a thorough understanding of the position we are in and is confident. That makes it easier for me to surrender my earlier concerns.

Appointment days drain my energy. Once I get the information, I process it through my tears. Then, I get my questions addressed and move on to process it all before the next appointment.

January 29th, 2020

The days are long because of all the prep ahead of each appointment, the mental preparations, getting to the office or hospital, processing all the emotions I'm dealing with, and then relaying that information to my family and friends. Some days, the mental load feels like the most challenging part. It takes me the rest of the day to unwind after each appointment. There is no chill in this girl on those days. I'm wound tightly and uncomfortable in my own skin. I think that's natural, though. My body is not my own the way it was.

Lately, the best way for me to relax is to shower. I let the hot water roll down my shoulders and pretend that every worry is taken with it. I repeat to myself,

My job is to love my baby by caring for myself.

My job is to love my baby by caring for myself.

My job is to love my baby by caring for myself.

As I was saying the latest mantra out loud in the shower, I felt a strong kick, then another. I wonder if he can tell how much I love him, how hard I'm fighting for him. In my mind, I know that I can't control what happens. In my heart, I know I'd do anything to help him.

After the shower, the doctor called me to reassure me that his bladder was empty, and that's why they couldn't get a picture of it. The baby's fluid levels were normal, his urinary tract was normal, and nothing else changed in the Omphalocele. Also, he doesn't have fluid in his chest wall (ascites). This means there is no more concern for cardiac arrest while in utero. My peace is temporarily restored. The next date I need to get to is in just under three weeks.

"Imperfections are not inadequacies;
they are reminders we are all in this
together."

- Brene Brown

CHAPTER 13

Learning How to Carry the Weight of Hope

I used to think that the challenges you face occur in order to teach us something we don't know about ourselves. Now, I'm not as sure. Being told that my pregnancy was high risk and that I could lose my son at any moment took me over half my pregnancy to digest. I spent months using every ounce of energy I had to find some semblance of hope. The best way forward was the next step. During those months, I abandoned making any plans. I don't mean that I wouldn't make plans with friends, but plans for how this pregnancy would go, plans for the future of our son. It was too much to bear – a plan meant hope, and hope was something I wasn't brave enough to carry. It felt too heavy at the time.

Hope can be lost and stolen. This lesson may be easy to understand, but my OCD-like tendencies and mechanisms made me a wreck because of how out of control every circumstance of my life felt. Before pregnancy, my OCD would make an appearance in the form of a 13-minute long shower (exactly), or it would feel like my world was ending. I had a ritual of applying chapstick from my nightstand before bed because the feeling of chapped lips was something I couldn't stop focusing on to complete tasks throughout the day. During my pregnancy, I knew that I had to reprioritize what I could control and not let my OCD run the show if I could help it.

I started to notice even the slightest change in my course throughout the day. These changes caused catastrophic uncertainty that I couldn't shake. I was also under the incorrect assumption that you could only hope if the circumstances were perfect. It's easy to hope life will go a certain way if that's the only way it's ever gone. Again, the revelations aren't earth-shattering to anyone who has lived a little, but that was a realization that surprised me.

You can't wish that a lifelong need for control goes away on its own. You can't think your way out of it. My way out looked like surrendering to something bigger than myself and noticing the small wins. Fighting for myself looked like scavenging for glimpses of goodness as much as I possibly could. I reminded myself every day I woke up still pregnant; what a blessing that was. I would celebrate excitedly at the first snowfall of winter, the first time I felt our son kick, or an uneventful ultrasound. In some ways, I lowered my expectations – well, in many ways. I knew before that life would never be perfect, but before this pregnancy, I could at least pretend that with a little more work or a little more time, my life would look exactly how I wanted it to. My pregnancy only amplified the fact that I was not being honest with myself. Perfection was never going to come. But, a colossal tradeoff of that realization is that my life had the potential to look like I wanted it to – if I was willing to see it for what it already was. I had to stop striving for some imaginary future happiness and learn to abide in the goodness of the present moment.

The timing of that realization could not have been more immaculate as the world was about to enter a global pandemic. Life was about to get more challenging for everyone.

February 3rd, 2020

The nurse's office started to see an uptick in the number of ill students. Wendy and I discussed that the best way to prevent me from catching whatever was going around was for me to spend more time downstairs in the special needs room of the school. She sacrificed her health for mine during that time to limit my exposure, I was so thankful for her. I was already anxious about this pregnancy, and now there is added anxiety about contracting something that could pass on to the baby, rendering us both weak.

The school staff all notice the cute baby bump that gets rounder by the day. I'm no longer trying to hide it. Honestly, it feels better to wear it proudly. They are generous with their compliments and well wishes.

This past weekend, I spent some time with my sister-in-law, Lexi. She was able to feel the baby kick for the first time.

Tomorrow, I have another appointment with my OBGYN. I plan on mentioning my heartburn, headaches, and nausea to her. I've also been dealing with a heavier mental load. I'm still grateful our son is growing and that we are surrounded by love.

My next ultrasound is in seventeen days in Pittsburgh. The hospital there gets the best pictures for us. The number of details we get from ultrasounds always amazes me. We can see his hair! I'm excited to see if it is growing and flowing the way it was last time. The ultrasound techs there are nice, but I prefer to see Nicole up here in our hometown. I feel at ease with her. It makes me hope that she can meet our son because of the enormous role she has already played in his life.

I've been thinking about names again. That is a good sign that hope is present.

February 3rd, 2020

I can't wait to choose his name! I won't accept anything less than perfection for his name. It will be his name for life — forever.

For now, my days are busy. Slow days cause my mind to wander. A wandering mind always finds its way to worry. I rely heavily on my daily devotionals. I've been journaling my thoughts after each day's lesson and growing closer to others who are doing them at the same time. I have noticed personal progress from the start of my journal to now. The consistent habit of choosing to see the good when I can and allowing the waves of bad to wash over me is affecting my overall disposition for the better.

Dylan and I can't be intimate, but we find other ways to connect on a personal level. One of those ways is to shower together. It's funny to me that when I shower alone, it's usually my time to cry out every emotion I'm feeling, but when Dylan and I shower together, I end up laughing harder than I ever do.

His optimism is the balance to my negativity. He's always there to interrupt my doom clouds with light and humor.

February 5th, 2020

I prepared my questions before last night's appointment and had a realization. Considering this is a high-risk pregnancy with an abnormal medical issue, I've had a good amount of normalcy. I know comparison is the thief of joy, but in this case, I am noticing that my journey seems to be more positive than some of the other stories I see.

My weight is up to 171 pounds. The doctor explained that the symptoms I asked her about were normal for me to experience.

February 5th, 2020

Our son's heart rate was 141, which was within the normal range. Of course, I am grateful that nothing was out of place, but I'm learning firsthand how much of a baddie you have to be to do this thing. Next time I see another pregnant woman, I'm going to give her the look you give someone when you know what they are going through.

You know, the subtle nod, eye contact, and the squinted eyes that say, "Look at you, momma. You are a beast!"

I've been reflecting on death more lately and how it is typically unpredictable. Few of us know the specific details of when, where, or how it happens. Yet it's the thread that connects all of us. Our mortality. The only way I can make sense of all that death ends is knowing that death is not the end. It's a change or transition. You don't have to agree with the premise of my faith, but that's where mine starts — at the end of what can be predicted or controlled. Everything else is an educated guess.

I've been trying to replace the fear in my mind that our son won't make it to his first breath or his first birthday with the hope that even if he doesn't, he will be at peace. I believe in Heaven, of course, but even if Heaven didn't exist, I feel certain our son could live happily in all the love I have for him.

Fear tries to have its way with me daily. All I know is that when I look back on this time, I want to say with certainty that I walked with fear, but I kept walking.

In the meantime, I continue to eat healthy, exercise, see the chiropractor, get massages, read devotions, and journal daily. I envision our son alive and thriving. That's an important part of my faith. I have to believe he will be in our arms; our perfect son will get to see our faces smiling at him. He certainly kicks like a warrior!

February 5th, 2020

I'm at twenty-five weeks. Dylan has been more eager to join the countdown lately. He keeps telling me, "I want him here so badly." I can't describe how much that uplifts me.

February 12th, 2020

It's been about a week since my last update. Most people know about not just my pregnancy but the issues surrounding it. It's not something I want to hide, but it does get tiring to repeat my explanations. My sleep, if you can call it sleep, has been awful — downright awful.

If it's not the headaches and nausea, it's the racing thoughts. I can't get my mind to shut up and stop running. Because of this, I'm not myself. The smallest inconvenience can stir up my emotions. I'm starting to feel imbalanced because of it.

In eight days, I get to see the little man again. I call him my sweet, handsome boy. Because of the exhaustion, I'm not hitting all my goals of self-care, but the effort is still very much in play.

I'm at twenty-five weeks now and starting to dream about how our son will be. What will he look like? Who will he resemble? I already know he will be a fighter. Every kick or baby punch is a reminder that I'm grateful I gave him a chance to show us what he's made of. I feel confident in my choice.

Each passing day reminds me that Dylan is close to seeing his son as well. I can't wait to see him as a dad. I know he'll be the absolute best. He proves it daily in the way he listens to every concern I have. You know how teenage girls make a list of their perfect man and then look back on it years later only to find how much their list changed as they matured?

February 12th, 2020

I am confident God has given me a man who would fit the list through every stage of my life. God has given me this child and the hope of our future together.

The week has been heavier than my usual week, but I am looking forward to a refreshing weekend with my family and friends. Saturday, Dylan and I are going to visit his sister, his parents, and my parents.

Sunday, my one best friend Erin and I will have some girl time together, and I look forward to that. She, along with my other best friend, Josephine, sent me the most caring messages on my worst days. Half the time, they don't realize the extent of what I'm going through, and I'll hear a ding from my cell phone only to see it's an encouraging message from one of them. Those are the types of friends I think everyone deserves. I am blessed to have them. You hold onto those who stand in your corner and come along for the ride no matter if the destination is unknown.

The way time is moving along at a steady pace has me starting to look into a place to stay after the baby is born and I'm discharged from the hospital. The Ronald McDonald House is an option through Grady's Decision. The organization sets up parents of children in apartments or hotels connected to or close to the hospital for a discounted price. It's a vital resource to any parent who wants to remain close to their child but can't stay in the room while they are in the hospital. I am looking into getting this assistance for Dylan and me because the doctors told us to anticipate that our son will need time in the NICU after delivery. We don't know how much time, but that's another problem for another day. At the present moment, I'm going to light a few lavender candles and eat some pistachios to see if it will help me sleep. I'd do almost anything for a good night's rest.

"God has not been trying an experiment on my faith or love in order to find out their quality. He knew it already. It was I who didn't. In this trial, He makes us occupy the dock, the witness box, and the bench all at once. He always knew that my temple was a house of cards. His only way of making me realize the fact was to knock it down."

- C.S. Lewis

CHAPTER 14

I Can't Do This, But I Am

In the meantime, I wrote a letter to give to our son when he turns eighteen. I wrote the name I hoped we would call him, and I let it all out. I had to embrace what an out-of-the-box task this was, and it helped me release some bottled-up emotions.

It took me a long time to gather my thoughts for what I would write – especially since I had to write from a place of hope and belief that he would reach that milestone. Then, it all just flowed. I am proud of myself for accomplishing that task. I can't overstate how proud I am to be his mother. I can't wait to watch him grow. I would shout this from the top of every building in town if necessary. I sealed it shut. I can't wait to hand him the letter on his eighteenth birthday, but for now, it is tucked away in our safe.

February 14th, 2020

My older sister, Chelcee, is pregnant. I'm so excited for her. At the same time, there is a concern in the back of my mind about how I will handle it if our son passes away. Of course, I will love my niece or nephew, but I'm afraid of being too distraught to be able to enjoy him or her fully. In a perfect world, our children will grow up together, so I'm willing to believe in that reality.

Today, I feel defeated for myself and, at the same time, excited for Chelcee. It is a relief that I no longer have to go through this pregnancy alone. I've always looked up to my big sister. It makes me wonder if I will have the opportunity to comfort her during her pregnancy as much as she has been a comfort to me.

I don't wish a high-risk pregnancy on anyone, but I am grateful for the unique perspective it has afforded me. I intend to help others navigate this. I'm also hoping that Chelcee leans into the joy of her pregnancy fully without worrying about any jealousy I am having. It's difficult not to feel some sadness — I'm only human, but in no way should that diminish someone else's joy.

Nervousness crept up this week as I anticipate going to Pittsburgh next week, but I'm ready to see our baby again. I look forward to and dread these appointments. I'm carrying the duality of my situation with all the strength I have, wondering if it will ever feel like the joy and fear will cancel each other out.

Dylan tells me every day how beautiful I am even as I'm starting to feel less and less worthy of the compliment. He tells me how much he loves me pregnant, how much I glow. I don't always believe him, but I believe he believes it.

February 14th, 2020

I had a strange thought today that even though I've been through so much, I feel like I can do this again. This journey didn't diminish my desire for more children. If anything, it's amplified. I've seen all that I'm willing to do for the love of my child, so I am convinced I will feel the same way about any future blessings that come.

After our son is born, he will have blood drawn for genetic testing. It will take some time before we get the results, but it's an essential part of his medical care. The results will help us understand how to best care for our son. When concern starts to emerge about that testing, I pray that nothing unexpected shows up.

I also imagine the bond our son will have with now two cousins who will be born around the same time as him. There's always something to be thankful for.

February 17th, 2020

This past Saturday, Dylan and I went to a birthday party for triplets. I found myself getting emotional watching the children run around and play at the party. I started to think about if our son will be running someday at another child's party or if he lives, what capacity will he have to enjoy these simple pleasures? It aggravates me to think this way instead of being grateful all the kids are healthy and happy.

Dylan is more reserved when out in public situations. I've always known this about him and can accept it most days. However, because of my elevated emotions, I took his silence at the party personally. I felt isolated with my thoughts, and because I was angry at him (for just being himself — I know), I didn't talk to him either. It all boiled over when we got back to the truck. I verbally processed all that I was feeling in a fit of tears.

February 17th, 2020

I couldn't stand how alone I felt at the moment. Thankfully, we ended the fight and made our way to the next family gathering a few towns away. When we left there, Dylan backed the truck into a light pole. I was surprised at how calm I was at that, considering how upset I was earlier. Maybe I got it all out!

The realization set in that his truck could be fixed. Yes, we will have to make the annoying call to process a claim through our insurance, but that felt manageable somehow. When I think about our life so far, everything is manageable — perhaps not ideal — but manageable. I'm going to try to keep that in mind. My self-reflection continued on the topic as I asked myself, Did we want the perfect pregnancy? Of course! No one hopes for adversity, but many have to manage it. I liken it to swimming in the ocean — the waves aren't all the same size. Sometimes a big-ass wave comes and knocks you over. Your instinct isn't to give up and drown. You get yourself back up to the surface, gulp the air, and keep swimming.

Faith is not easy to practice, but it's been an essential part of the reason both Dylan and I are still standing. We have always made a great team. We are opposite in complementary ways. Where I am weak, he is strong, and vice versa. He is easily my best friend. Together, we cleaned the living room on Saturday and rearranged the furniture. It looks huge now. I'm looking forward to our next appointment on Thursday. My phone calendar lights up like Times Square every time I open it. I'm booked for the foreseeable future with medical appointments. On the long drive to Pittsburgh, I sing the whole way. Dylan always says, "Sing away, Shelb." I sing so I don't worry, so I don't cry, so our son can hear his mom doing something she loves. Saturday, I said out loud to my reflection in the bathroom mirror, "I can't do this," but today is Monday, and look who is still doing this.

"All you can change is yourself,
but sometimes that changes
everything."

– Gary W. Goldstein

CHAPTER 15

Finding Inspiration

A strange quirk that helped me through this pregnancy was finding inspirational quotes. I started a habit that helped immensely. On days when I could feel myself descending into some fresh worry, I would open my phone, click on Pinterest, and look up a quote. Then I'd say to myself, "Today, I will live my life based on this quote." I closed my eyes and slid the cursor up and down before placing my other finger down randomly on the screen. It was a strange way to boost my dopamine, and often, the quote I landed on surprised me by how relevant it was. Sometimes, I would find a post or article that would lead me to self-reflect or adjust my thinking about a topic I rarely considered. They weren't all pregnancy-related, either, and that helped give my mind a break from what I thought about all the other waking moments.

I learned if you are going to ask God for a sign (and in those days, I was begging him for one), you also need to go looking for His answer.

You wouldn't ask someone for directions and then keep your eyes closed the rest of the way, would you? When I land on a positive quote, it encourages me. When I land on a sad quote, it makes me realize I don't own the right to discomfort. We each have our burden to carry.

The quotes became anchors for me. My search history looked like "pregnancy affirmations, grace, strength, etc..." It may seem silly to some, but I found out when I pushed my pride away that it doesn't take much to talk your mind into a better way of thinking.

February 18th, 2020

We have an appointment to meet the delivery team in twenty-eight days exactly.

Today is Dylan's birthday. He is twenty-five and as handsome as ever. We have been a part of each other's lives since we were eighteen. I get excited thinking about all the future birthdays we will celebrate together. Since our appointment is today, I hope we get the good news I wished to receive for my birthday. That would be the best present. I'm excited to get another round of pictures and to see how much our son has grown. I'm praying the brain and lungs continue to develop. My devotional today was about not worrying by giving all of our cares to God. I know I've mentioned it forty thousand times, but I struggle with not having control. The Moms of Omphaloceles page helps in this regard. I connected with another mom there whose due date is about three days from mine. She gave me a dose of reality that I desperately needed at that moment. She reminded me that no matter what the outcome is, we will get to hold and kiss these little ones we are both fighting so hard for. It's another well-timed reminder that we are not alone in this fight.

Dylan and I have grown closer than ever through this experience as well. Our relationship is rapidly gaining a depth I couldn't have fathomed. I thought I loved him more than I ever would on our wedding day, but that love continues to grow. I married my best friend. He has the most genuine love of anyone I have ever met. I could stare at the speck in his right eye all day. Even his imperfections are beautiful to me. His arms are my home. Some days, they are all I am fighting to return to. The way he joins me and holds my hand at every ultrasound — the only other person in the room who knows every detail of my anxiety — is the only one who calms it right out of me. I see every possible future when I look at him, and I love each one.

February 24th, 2020

Today's appointment was fantastic. It was awesome. The baby weighed 2 pounds, 5 ounces. He is doing well, tucked safely inside the womb. He's weighing in the 38th percentile, which means his growth has slowed a little, but he's still reading on the charts. His left kidney is measuring 2/10 of a millimeter larger than normal, but for some reason, I'm not overly stressed about it. I'm just relieved that he's still growing.

We met a new doctor who reminded us that it is common for Omphalocele kids to have chromosomal issues. It's another consideration I hold, but I don't have space to let it consume me. His face is so beautiful. I can tell he looks just like his dad. I looked at the ultrasound screen and talked to our son, saying, "We've come so far, little man. Only eleven weeks to go, and you'll be here with us."

Later that night, I was scrolling through posts on Facebook, and a video came up of a pregnant woman documenting the joy of her pregnancy. I tear up every time I see stuff like that. The part of me that was desperate for our son to have no health concerns is the part of me that feels most fragile. It made me run to the latest ultrasound pictures. I examined our son's face, looking for signs of a complicated genetic issue. Could more be wrong with him? Will genetic testing give us more to worry about or ease our minds? How long will I last when every day — every hour — has me careening between feelings of empowerment and feelings of total helplessness?

Dylan and I agreed to stick to being adamant we get the bloodwork to see if something further is wrong with the baby, but only once he is born, not during the pregnancy through Amniocentesis. The genetic doctor we met with was pushing this procedure on us.

February 24th, 2020

Amniocentesis is a procedure that could be a possible cause of preterm labor, a risk I refused to take. Having the amniocentesis procedure done would mean that we could know before delivery what exactly our son would be facing other than his Omphalocele. The doctor voiced his concerns and then once again reminded us that due to his birth defect and the severity we still could decide to abort him.

Dylan and I had to come together to decide if the risks of this procedure outweighed the benefits. Nothing would change in the care of our son once he is born. All teams of the hospital would be available regardless, so why take the pre-term labor risk? We continued with the pregnancy and refused the extra testing and, once again, the abortion.

We stood by the choices we made, strongly, and best of all, together.

I will be twenty-eight weeks on Wednesday. That is mind-boggling to me.

Sleep these days is mostly non-existent. If you know anything about me, understand this: I value my sleep. I need sleep to function at a baseline level. Without it, I'm weaker emotionally and physically. I walk around half-human, half-zombie. The situation becomes more dire by the day. All I want is to be held by Dylan and to sleep.

"For I know the plans I have for you," declares the Lord, "plans to prosper you and not harm you, plans to give you hope and a future..."

- Jeremiah 29:11

CHAPTER 16

Our First Funeral in a Global Pandemic

March 2nd, 2020

I'm an emotional wreck. Just as the hope in me was building and my pregnancy appeared to be getting on the right track, the whole world stopped. Coronavirus is in full force, and while most of the world avoids public life at home, the hospitals are overflowing with COVID patients and schools with Fifths Disease, Strep, and other respiratory illnesses. I have a new fear that my son will contract a virus and won't survive. I've been taking each moment as it comes and living in the present as a survival tactic for so long; it's only now that I'm starting to consider what our life will look like once he arrives. He's got a ninety percent chance of living, which are great odds, and a fantastic medical team. I'm leaning on the hope that he will not only live but thrive.

In order to ensure that, he will need to stay safe inside my womb until my due date. That is my focus. It's my biggest concern because it gives him the greatest chance at thriving.

I've also been thinking about my planned C-section. I am struggling to accept that it is necessary. I have chronically low blood pressure, and I fear that I won't survive it. My fears constantly consume me. Dylan must be overwhelmed by me. I'm trying to lean on my faith and strengthen my inner thoughts. I'm employing all the tactics I have, but this is so hard. I'm starting to feel myself slipping and am afraid of the person this pregnancy is making of me. Will I be this way, riddled with anxiety and constantly trying to save myself from it if I get pregnant again? I'm afraid of losing the baby and fearful of losing myself.

March 5th, 2020

Dylan and I had a long cry together last night. We let out some pent-up frustration and fear we each had. It's work carrying this burden together. We don't want to create more of a burden for the other by the ways we aren't coping well. I madly love him and his baby — our baby. I want it to work out with every bit of my intention. I'm reminding myself we are on the same team. We are fighting for the same future.

Each ultrasound feels like we are seeing our son through a window. He's our perfect human. The size of his Omphalocele measures 6.8 centimeters by 5.2 centimeters by 6 centimeters. It contains his entire liver, which is much larger than others. The doctors told us that it's not only large on the measurement scale but also large for his gestational age and size as well. I will ask the surgeon to explain in further detail what this means exactly.

Dylan's grandfather is not doing well, which is adding to our worries. No one in the family wants to lose him, but especially because we lost Nan so recently. There seems to be a wall of loss closing in around us. My mind is well-acquainted with death lately. It's like he's sitting at the back of my consciousness, threatening everyone I love.

I'm trying to remain strong for Dylan so that I can be a safe place for him to express what he's going through. In less than seventy days, we should be meeting our little warrior son. The image of holding him in our arms and getting to sing our love over him is what's getting me through.

My emotions continue to be scattered, ready to change faster than I know why I feel any certain way. My body is unrecognizable, as is my mind. I cry less in the shower, though. Does this mean I can't possibly feel anymore? That I got them all out?

March 5th, 2020

It always helps me to meet up with friends from the Omphalocele group.

I had dinner with Carrie the other night. I am grateful for her because she never holds back when responding to the thousands of questions I have at any given moment. She is generous with her honesty and still finds a way to make the hard truths feel safe. She and her daughter are priceless to me.

Our next appointment is in twelve days. Each period of days between appointments, I focus on eating healthy, praying, and controlling what I can.

My next project, which is part distraction, part trusting in the process, is to get the nursery ready. I am hoping to tackle that this upcoming weekend. We ordered the last of the baby items needed to complete his nursery.

March 6th, 2020

We received word today that Pa is in his last days. We went to see him and our family to say our last goodbyes. No one was ready for this. Family members on Dylan's side filled Pa's room. All of us were there to send him off, knowing he would go in our love. I was at his bedside talking to him and praying to myself that he would give us one more smart comment before leaving. He did not. When we got the news that he had passed, I prayed this time to him, asking him to be another guardian for our son.

March 7th, 2020

Dylan got a haircut in preparation for his grandfather's funeral and viewing. I hate to see him lose his family members. My heart breaks for him.

March 8th, 2020

Today was the start of my preterm false labor. With everything else going on, the stress is getting to me.

March 9th, 2020

I'm having more pain in my lower pelvis and a ton of cramping. I called my OB because I was concerned it was preterm labor. She told me to drink lots of fluids today and inform her if anything changes. It was an uneasy day on top of the grieving we were doing for Dylan's grandpa.

March 11th, 2020

I'm having contractions. Possible Braxton Hicks. I have a sudden overwhelming realization that I have no clue if they are the real deal or Braxton Hicks. Today is the viewing for Pa, Dylan's grandfather. It is a struggle for me to keep myself calm and try to be a shoulder for Dylan with the pain I'm in. Still, I know Dylan is hurting as well. We are both grieving that Pa won't get to meet his first great-grandson.

March 12th, 2020

Pa's funeral was today. I stood above his casket and promised him I would tell our son about the legacy of love he left behind. He had a quick cleverness and a witty spirit. Taking minor jabs at us was his signature. He always called me the "Blonde Zimmerman." He gave the best hugs even though there were times he probably didn't want to be hugged. He faced all the risks of heart surgery and weighed the balance to be a part of his grandkids' lives a little longer. He was as stubborn as they come but had an unmatched heart. I will never forget him holding Nan's hand in their recliners through the end of her life. I'm so glad they are together again; I find so much peace in knowing that.

The weather was beautiful but windy. Our entire small town seemed to show up to send him off. The outpouring was incredibly heartwarming to us. His pallbearers, most of whom were Pas' very own loved ones, looked regal in their dress blues.

I'm so proud of Dylan and his family for the way they carried themselves through such a difficult time.

"They asked her, "How do you get through tough moments?" She answered, "Do not trust the way you see yourself when your mind is in turbulence, and remember that even pain is temporary. Honor your boundaries, treat yourself gently, let go of perfection, and feel your emotions without letting them control you. You have enough experience to face the storm and evolve from it.""

— Yung Pueblo

CHAPTER 17

Mind Over Matter Sometimes Looks Like Medication Over Meditation

Have you ever looked back on a trial in your life and wondered how you made it through? It's as if the person you were during that time was someone you don't recognize, someone you admire, someone you wonder whether they are still present with you, waiting to come out the next time they are needed.

I often look back on the pregnancy and wonder how I didn't swing from one depressive episode to the next. You can track the grief I experienced throughout this entire book. It was an ever-present frenemy. I describe it like that because, as uncomfortable as grief was, it drew me closer to God and led me to some incredible resources. Walking with grief was also the key to a more mature and stable place for me mentally. Grief and growth don't always go together. I'm grateful for the resources that helped ensure my grief didn't break me open.

I always loved the quote, "Mind over matter." It was a lucky pebble I kept with me when needed. I knew the key to winning the battle over my situation had to start in my mind.

I mentioned earlier in this memoir that I was previously diagnosed with OCD, depression, and anxiety through my family doctor, but I've seen a handful of therapists since turning eighteen to help manage those. I saw a cognitive behavior therapist who helped give me valuable tools and tricks to manage my issues. My more formidable enemy has always been the feeling that I'm not in control. What feels sad or frustrating to others used to cripple me with anxiety and make me ill. Behind my need for control was a massive fear that if I stopped looking at what could happen, the worst *would* happen.

I say all of that because it was only through a mixture of growing closer to God, the support of my friends and family, and cognitive behavioral therapy that gave me the perspective that my fears were unwarranted most of the time. By the time the worst did happen to me, I had enough in my arsenal to tackle each worry and concern that came along.

At this point in my pregnancy, I was doing everything I could to avoid going into preterm labor. I stayed hydrated, prayed, and even read My First Bible to our son at night while lying in bed next to my husband.

I kept reflecting on the different person I had become from the beginning of it to now. In the early days of this pregnancy, I went into fight mode for a handful of weeks. There was a constant pull from the most negative sides of myself to wallow and sink. Every positive thought or inch of forward progress felt like a hard-earned battle.

I started to play a game against myself. If I had one negative thought, I could counter it with two positive thoughts. For example, one day, I had the thought:

My body failed this baby by not correctly developing his body.

I replaced that negative thought with two positives:

My body is a safe space for this child.
My body is incredible for housing a life.

I think learning to deal with intrusive and negative thoughts at an early age prepared me for this moment. Even so, I could have used a little therapy boost, given all that I was carrying (both literally and figuratively) at the time.

Towards the late side of the middle of my pregnancy, I contacted a hypnotist from a town over. Despite my initial skepticism, it became invaluable to me. We had a brief interview on the phone, and she helped me decide on what type of hypnosis and visualization would best serve my needs. It worked so well for me that I used her regularly for the last five weeks of my pregnancy. The techniques she taught me got me through times when it got harder to breathe, during my preterm labor, and especially during the C-section. It's just another tool to have in the box if you want it. As unbelievable as hypnosis may sound, it's simply a way to channel a different part of your brain and tap into your meditative mind space. It was a total game-changer for me.

As a nurse, I'm also a firm believer in the benefits of being well-medicated. I was on Zoloft for a handful of years. Zoloft is what's called an SSRI, or serotonin reuptake inhibitor. In short, it gives your brain a boost of feel-good hormones to regulate your mood. It helped me through a major depressive period in my life a few too many years after my grandfather passed away. I was as close to him as a best friend, but there were other circumstances in my life during that time that I wasn't able to conquer on my own. I also struggled with racing thoughts.

Right around the time I was twenty-nine weeks along, my preterm labor started. Omphalocele babies sometimes stop growing inside the womb because they run out of space. The doctors believe it was caused by stress and likely had a variety of other causes contributing to it, but they could pinpoint nothing as the culprit. The medical team gave me fluids and had me sit in a jacuzzi tub to relax the contractions. Once the contractions shrank back down to a safe level, I was able to continue my pregnancy. For some reason, I kept the day's events to myself. I didn't tell Dylan I was sitting in the hospital. At the time, I was terrified they would have to med-flight me to Pittsburgh to deliver the baby. Reflecting on that decision, I know how irresponsible it was – both to take on the entire burden by myself and to keep my husband in the dark. When I went to the hospital, in all the pain I was in from having the contractions, I was mad at myself. I blamed my body for what was happening. I needed someone there in that hospital to reassure me it wasn't my fault, but I was the one shutting that possibility out. If I had been open with my husband, my mother, or even my sister, who worked across the street from the OB ward, I would have had someone to hold my hand through it all. I encourage anyone going through a similar situation to learn from my mistakes.

March 10th, 2020

I woke up all night! I woke up at 2:00 a.m., 4:00 a.m., 6:00 a.m., and 7:00 a.m. in pain. Every twenty minutes, I felt significant pressure and pain. I knew something wasn't right, and the first thing my mind told me to do was pray. I prayed this wasn't an instance of preterm labor and that our son wouldn't be stillborn.

I went to work that morning after an awful night's sleep, and my coworker, Nicole M., thought my pain was more than Braxton Hicks, and she kindly encouraged me to go to the hospital. I began to sob but knew this was the best choice.

The staff at the school offered to drive me and dropped me off near the emergency room entrance to get into the OB ward. I was thankful to be there. I explained to the maternity nurses what was going on and changed into a lovely hospital gown. Several nurses familiar with my history came to check on me — each one asking me why I was alone. I didn't have an answer for them. The bolus of IV fluids did little to help. I explained to the nurses I was already hydrated on the orders of my regular OBGYN. At this point, my fears overwhelmed me. I was completely alone and didn't understand why I didn't call Dylan or my Mom. I think I didn't want to admit it was happening. The hospital staff got me into the jacuzzi tub to help me relax. I was praying the whole time in my mind for God to help me keep this baby safe and make it to my delivery date. The contractions were causing me increased pain and coming on faster, occurring every one to two minutes.

I couldn't handle being alone in this anymore, and a nurse highly encouraged me to tell my partner, so I called Dylan to tell him what was going on.

March 10th, 2020

My mom and sister were the next to learn I was in the maternity ward, and they were in that hospital quicker than I thought possible. I was beside myself wishing these were Braxton hicks or anything other than preterm labor.

After the contractions were under control and the doctors verified that I was not dilated, I was able to go home. There was intense deliberation between the doctors about whether or not they should airlift me to Pittsburgh to be on the safe side, but I am grateful it didn't come to that. A wave of relief washed over me after the ordeal was over.

I know how lucky I was not to be airlifted. It was such a close call, and my stubbornness could have gotten me in much more trouble.

This experience made me realize how often I choose to face trouble alone. Thinking back, I have always been this way, and I don't know why. It feels like who I am. I don't like to feel like my problems are dragging others down. I also have trouble telling the difference between wanting something and needing it. Even if I ask a confidante for advice, I'll listen thoroughly, but I rarely take it.

As much as I need reassurance, a part of me wants to be strong and independent. There are times when I feel isolated, even as others are offering their help. In the darkest parts of myself, I admit that no one can help my circumstances; nobody can change the outcome of this pregnancy — not even me.

"Proud. I'm so proud of you. I'm proud that you keep showing up every single day. I'm so proud of all the tough decisions you had to make, and even though it was hard, you stood your ground. I'm proud that you never gave up on yourself and kept fighting for everything you love. I'm proud that despite everything you've been through, you still wake up and find ways to smile every day. I'm proud of you and how far you've come, and I'm even more excited for everything that's still to come."

— Nikki Banas

CHAPTER 18

Making It Through The Second Half of March

March 13th, 2020

Today, the OBGYN re-assessed me for dilation and continued signs of labor to make sure it entirely stopped after our scare from three days ago. Dylan was able to come with me. I'm glad I don't have to do this alone. This upcoming Tuesday, we have another ultrasound in Pittsburgh.

Dylan and I are still grieving the loss of his grandfather, whom we call Pa. The way the firefighters and EMS volunteers showed their love and support impressed me. They came out in droves to pay their respects and condolences. If our son joins the local Volunteer Fire Department, he will be the fourth generation on his father's line to do so.

My work halted for two more weeks due to the COVID-19 pandemic. We worked from home while waiting to see if we could return to in-school education. The staff members at our school are sending video messages to the kids with words of encouragement so they don't feel as isolated. It is isolating to sit home alone, worrying about what havoc the virus is capable of. The news is not a source of comfort on that front. The death toll continues to rise, and I fall into the category of those in the highest-risk group.

We lived in a different world the day we told Nan and Pa we were pregnant. I remember Pa telling us that he thought it was a boy. He jabbed Dylan, saying he could only give him great-grandsons. I never got to tell my grandma about it. I've been missing all three of them even more in my isolation and praying for them to watch over us more now than ever. Dylan and I just weren't ready for them to pass away. The pain of it is unbearable at times. I keep praying for God to strengthen our son's lungs and for continued help getting us all safely to my due date. We already know he is strong.

March 21st, 2020

Our appointment on March 17th was a lot to take in, as most of them are lately. He weighed in at approximately 3 pounds, 8 ounces. He is starting to take practice breaths, and there were no further issues. His Omphalocele measures roughly 7 centimeters by 6 centimeters by 5 centimeters, which means there has been no significant growth of it since our last appointment. It is still just his liver in there, but the doctors are concerned there may be some intestines in it also. If this is the case, his post-birth care will be that much more difficult.

I met my new maternal-fetal medicine doctor. She was kind and added iron supplements because my labs were low. We also met the neonatologist. She was also sweet, but it was scary to meet with her because she had to lay out the specifics of the plans for our delivery day. She didn't sugarcoat the situation. The closer we get to meeting our son, the more real it becomes.

The hospital looks vastly different from my last appointment. Everyone is wearing masks and gloves. If someone coughs or sneezes, all the eyes in the room shift to that person. I barely breathe in rooms with other people; I'm too scared of contracting something this late in the pregnancy. I'm not afraid for myself but for our son.

The doctors told us we would be lucky if we got to see our son for five minutes after he was born. Their biggest medical concern is that his organs function and lungs work. I couldn't stop crying after hearing that. I'd spent so much time just trying to make it to my delivery date, but it hadn't occurred to me that after all this, vital parts of him may not work. While I was crying, I kept thinking, all I want is for him to survive.

March 21st, 2020

I never let the doctors see me undone the way I did at that appointment. I felt the walls caving in on me and wanted nothing more than to escape this appointment and go home. The medical team sat Dylan and me in a conference room and, one by one, went over every painfully necessary part of their plan to give our son the best possible chance. It was too much for my weary heart to take. They will have to take him from me immediately after delivery, and there is a chance I won't be able to see or touch him for several days. There is also a real possibility that they will have to revive him in the room after pulling him out. Our meeting left no place for skimping on the details. I realize why they had to share what they did, but it was overwhelming. I'm balancing my love and fear the best I can. I love this little boy so much! He has to beat the odds we're up against. He has to!

The surgeon who will perform his closure surgery was thrilled by our son's growth and overall health. She believes his ultrasounds are reassuring. I'm glad she is hopeful because I didn't go into that meeting feeling the same way. Each appointment provides the clarity I'm looking for. Because of the COVID precautions, only Dylan and I are allowed at the doctor's appointments from now on. I understand it, but it does make me sad because of how much of a blessing it has been so far to have my mom accompany me. I am focusing on what I do have.

I keep thinking of Dylan becoming a dad. I can't wait for him to meet our son. It will make all of this worth it — even as I'm recovering, Dylan will have that time alone to bond with our son. I couldn't be more impressed with how he has kept his composure throughout this ordeal.

March 21st, 2020

Each time I think of the ways Dylan has shown his strength and support of me, it makes me wish I could have been with him sooner.

We are close to deciding on our son's name. My first choice is Lincoln. My little Lincoln. It seems fitting to name him that, as during this pregnancy, I have fought hard to keep my head up through it all. Finding those heads-up pennies throughout this, he is forever my reminder to keep my head up in any circumstance or situation. I'm at thirty-two weeks and hoping he will weigh five pounds by the next doctor's appointment.

March 23rd, 2020

The only grocery store in town that provides pick-up services is a store called Martin's. We are grateful for this service because it allows us to be as safe as we can. Many of the items we usually buy are in short supply, so we could only get about a third of what we needed. We had to go without buns, milk, and Gatorade this week.

The dollar store had some of the items that Martin's did not. I'm glad that worked out in our favor. The last of the nursery items should be arriving soon.

It's a scary time — especially to be pregnant. Dylan and I stay inside ninety-five percent of the time. Neither of us is certain when work will begin again or when we will be returning to a forty-hour work week. We are unsure of many aspects of the future, which is just on brand for this entire pregnancy.

It makes me feel weak as the situation seems to get worse as more time passes. I can't seem to catch my breath. I never would have chosen these complications. Who would?

March 23rd, 2020

No one wants their baby to face struggles and surgeries before their first breaths on earth and beyond. The mental load of being bored and scared all the time made me realize how much I was using going to work as a way to keep my brain busy. Now that is gone, and once my work is completed at home, I feel I have all the time in the world to think about the worst-case scenarios.

The most exciting part of my days now is when our little man gets the hiccups. It makes me laugh every time. Does he know how much joy it brings me to know he's happy and safe in there?

The less exciting parts of my day involve taking iron supplements and counting down the days between each doctor's appointment.

My appointments are now shorter than before due to the new precautions. Now I also have to go alone, which causes some added stress. I don't feel safe anywhere but at home. In a way, though, this pregnancy does distract me from worrying about the virus at all times. It is punishing to be alone as much as we are these days. I miss hugging people most of all. I could really use a hug.

Yesterday, I lay on the couch and basked in the sun coming through the window. It was so warm and beneficial for my mental state.

Today's rainy weather is more in line with my internal state. It's gloomy, rainy, and a mess outside. I'm gloomy, teary, and a mess inside. Despite it all, I'm still finding a way to get up in the morning and a way to close my eyes at night — to give it all up for fitful rest. My fate is forever tied to Dylan and this baby. These are my two favorite humans. Counting the dog, we will be a family of four soon.

March 23rd, 2020

It's been an hour since I took my iron pill, and it's almost time to eat.

This babe must get bigger!

It's just another day stuck in the house we made into a home.

March 27th, 2020

As I write this, the efforts to curb a global pandemic are in full swing. The schools are closed, and some countries have shut down completely. Elective surgeries are canceled. In some hospitals, women have to give birth alone. I'm praying this does not happen to us. I know our son will need his dad there — mainly because I will be recovering after the C-section.

We had our first biophysical profile exam, or BPP, yesterday. Those tests are cutting-edge and will give the doctors responsible for our care an enormous amount of helpful information. The BPP test measures overall fetal health. It consists of two noninvasive tests, including fetal monitoring and ultrasound, and typically takes between thirty and seventy minutes to complete.

This biophysical profile helps practitioners observe the fetus's heart rate, breathing, movement, muscle tone, and amniotic fluid surrounding it in the womb. It also looks for fetal activity and calculates points based on the findings. Activities that add points include the fetus opening its mouth, movement in the arms and legs, and the way it twists and turns in utero. It also examines if babies are practicing breathing motions. If so, the score is higher. The higher the score, the better the outcomes typically are. These results are added together for a score that falls between zero and ten.

March 27th, 2020

A score between eight and ten is considered normal. A lower score suggests a possible problem that warrants a more thorough evaluation. A score of four or less requires significant monitoring up to possible induced labor.

Our son is cute as always and covered in hair. As I write this, he has another bout of hiccups. The doctors recommend I stay at home as much as I'm able to to reduce my risk of contracting any sickness. At this point in the pregnancy, we can't afford to take any chances.

I am still taking walks with my mom and niece. They contribute immensely to my mental health. For now, the reports say that outside is a safe place to be.

I am afraid for my sister Chelcee, who is also pregnant and still works in a hospital. One of my good friends had a miscarriage recently. It is heartbreaking. I question why this happened at a time like this. To honor her loss and the strength it will require for them to get through this time, I decided never to dwell in self-pity for as long as I can help it. I prayed for her to be comforted and hoped that she would be reunited with the child they lost in heaven someday.

I received a call from Magees Hospital informing me that I may end up delivering alone. ALONE! I don't know how anyone can be expected to do that. It concerns me that fathers could be robbed of those first moments with their children, and mothers are neglected the support that is so crucial to their well-being. It concerns me that Dylan may never know his son if his life ends in that delivery room and he doesn't survive delivery.

March 27th, 2020

Through all of the setbacks, I am surprised most by how little I cried over possibly delivering alone. It's partly due to having hope that the protocols will change by the time I deliver. Part of it is likely because so much has happened in these past months; I am not sure if there is any more space to grieve.

The gripping fear of miscarrying or delivering a stillborn child is now replaced with the fear of my son contracting a deadly virus after he is born that his body doesn't have the means to fight off.

I am looking forward to getting to hold him and look him in the face, for his ears to hear me tell him a thousand times a day that I love him, and for his eyes to start to recognize my face as he hears my voice. I wish I could imagine what it would be like to meet him for the first time, but it's all a mystery to me.

He is brave, strong, and so loved. I have to choose gratitude for the way God increased my capacity to love in his mysterious way. He taught me to hope by walking with me through a time of hopelessness and fear.

As always, Dylan is my rock. He and I both navigate the testing waters of a high-risk pregnancy, a hormonal siege, and all the uncertainty life has thrown our way since those two pink lines changed our worlds forever.

March 30th, 2020

Despite all the precautions we are taking to avoid contracting Covid, we were able to get ice cream. Life is weird. I remember the day we told my mom I was pregnant; we were in the Dairy Queen parking lot. All we felt at that time was excitement.

March 30th, 2020

I've been praying all week for our world as we continue to stay socially isolated at home. We finally got the rest of the nursery put together. It was less emotional than my last attempt. I almost felt numb about it. I took lots of pictures of Dylan building all of it for our memory book. The only other way I could contribute was to clean up the room and windows. The crib sheets we ordered are the last item on our list, and they are back-ordered. We still have time left, but it's still moving so fast.

I started reading a beginner Bible to the baby. I want him to hear God's stories while he rests safely inside of me. I set a goal to finish it before I give birth. If I remain on my schedule, I will finish the last chapter one day before he is born.

Life came full circle. I used to hate being home alone, and now I'm scared to leave. I'm trying to do everything I can in the best interests of our little family.

I packed my hospital bag and felt scared but prepared. I face every fear as it comes and am realizing it's a hurdle but not a wall. I'm not letting it stop me, even if it slows me down. In just forty-four days, Dylan and I will meet our son. The debate over his name is heating up. We will either name him Lincoln or Colson.

Each night, Dylan places his hands on my belly and wraps his arms around me. The habit is calming to me, and it gives both of us a chance to be close to one another while we withhold sexual intimacy. The peace of our closeness overcomes me. I sink into sleep, counting all the ways we long for this child and all our future children. Instead of counting sheep, I count the ways I want him to be the father of my children. I am convinced our married life should always be walked hand in hand through every circumstance, good and bad. With that conviction, I find my way to sleep again.

"To find yourself, think for yourself."

— Socrates

CHAPTER 19

Time Will Tell All

There was a time during my pregnancy when I felt pressured to have a baby shower, take maternity pictures, and do all the customary rituals related to a first pregnancy. I felt pressured to have the pregnancy glow and for my face to look like I was on cloud nine, riding a rainbow to a pot of maternal gold. Several friends mentioned these rites of passage, stating something about how "it's always been," and I need to express just how hard it was for me to decline a baby shower to protect my sanity. It seemed to be an impossible task for me to face my loved ones and pretend to celebrate something I wasn't sure would happen.

An aspect of pregnancy that isn't frequently discussed is the assumptions people make. The first assumption is that because you are telling them, you are excited. I was excited, but that was mixed with that premonition that something wasn't right.

The first consideration I had about a baby shower was the memory of how anxiety-inducing my bridal shower was. Of course, the second consideration came after our son's diagnosis – how could I face a room full of items we may not ever use? We didn't want to be wholly unprepared either, so an acceptable compromise was to keep a room with the essentials in our house with the doors closed.

The next unspoken rule of motherhood is the unsolicited advice given by everyone from your close family members to far-off acquaintances. The looks I got when I explained that I did not want a baby shower ranged from surprise to confusion to thinly veiled disgust. People didn't seem to realize I was not going through a normal pregnancy. Every choice I made was to protect my heart and mind. It didn't have to make sense to anyone else but me.

On top of that, I'm not fond of excess and clutter. I work best having what is essential and takes up minimal space.

April 3rd, 2020

We made it through another week without contracting COVID. Dylan and I are discussing the possibility of moving into the house he grew up in. It sounds like a good opportunity, but it might require more energy than we can take on. It also might be a welcome distraction.

Dylan isn't sure that he wants to live in the house where he grew up. There is plenty of potential to make new memories, and it is more conveniently located in our town than where we currently live. There is a part of me that is sentimental to our current house because of all the effort I put into making it ours. At least initially, the house would not feel like our own.

The primary concern in my mind is this baby, though, and I hope that he will be able to play in the front yard.

I had a second biophysical profile exam (BPP) — this time, I had to go alone. Masks were mandatory as well. My heart pounded from the second I left my car until I put it in reverse to come home. Sometimes, you would swear I'm not breathing the entire appointment. Each one, I'm fearful, will be the one I find out our baby is not alive. Most days are touch and go. The doctors allowed me to record his heartbeat today, though. I will treasure that moment forever.

I talked to my grandpa today, who told me out of the blue, "Everything is going to be all right with your baby; it'll all work out." The strange thing about that is we haven't told him the extent of our issues. We didn't want him to worry about us, so we didn't fill him in.

April 3rd, 2020

His comment to us made me reflect. In many ways, this pregnancy has gotten easier. For the first time in a while, I feel truly hopeful. I look at the Mothers Of Omphaloceles page, and I have hope. Even if he has to have a trach, be on ventilation for a short period, or require oxygen, I think he's going to live. I feel confident that our little one will make it. I'm sending him all the positive vibes and praising him for how strong he has been through it all. We have all been strong, haven't we?

I'm excited for our future as a family and hopeful for whatever the post-pandemic world looks like as well. It's gloomy out there, but I hope the other side makes us all love deeper. I hope that relationships are strengthened and that no one takes even the smallest joy for granted after this is all over. As for Dylan and me, our reality was changed four months before the rest of the world joined us in this foreign world we now face.

In this way, I feel ahead of the curve in learning some crucial life lessons. I no longer feel isolated in my despair (the whole world is despairing). It's not that I would wish for others to commiserate with me, just that I am grateful to have others to commiserate with.

To comfort myself, I sometimes list what I know. For now, I know I can't wait to become a parent with Dylan. I am looking forward to the possibility of moving to a new home, and I believe that it will all work out as it's supposed to.

Thinking about our family brings the biggest smile to my face. Having something to smile about makes me feel the presence and tender care of God the most.

April 6th, 2020

This weekend, Dylan and I were able to get out of the house for some fresh air. Because of the pandemic, he and I got to see more of each other in the last few weeks. I've been missing giving and receiving hugs from family members, though.

Chelcee, my sister, worked Saturday and was exposed to someone with COVID-19. Her test result was negative, but to be safe, she had wanted her daughter, Evelynn, to stay at our parents' house to not expose her to the virus.

I remain at home, working remotely. I can feel the different dynamic of working from home. While I still get to see the kids through pictures, I miss seeing them in person. I miss my friends from work, too.

I completed my FMLA form and set my last day to the Friday before our due date. This ensures I have the most time to spend with our son after he is born. It gives us the most cushion to be with him if he has an extended stay at the hospital.

Dylan and I put the two names we picked out into a hat and tried to choose that way. I have been calling him Lincoln in my head for so long, but I think Dylan is leaning toward Colson. I want it to be fair, and I want Dylan and I to both be happy with his name. If we name him Lincoln, his middle name will be Andrew. If we have another son, we can name that one Colson James. If our next child is a daughter, we'd like to name her Sophie Elaine Maree. Dylan dislikes three-part names, but I'm glad to have a plan. God is probably laughing at any plans I make either way, considering how little control any of us have.

I continue to pray that the pandemic restrictions are loosened within the next thirty-seven days to allow Dylan to be in the delivery room.

April 6th, 2020

I can imagine the sweet, chubby cheeks of our baby now. His first cries, piercing through the room — his entrance is going to be fierce!

I made myself laugh while thinking back on this pregnancy. I dare to admit I enjoyed being pregnant. It goes against most of what I have journaled so far, but it's true. Recording every fear and anxiety-ridden moment has allowed me the space I needed to process what I've been through so that the rest of my day could be spent moving forward. Also, it is easier to journal when you are feeling down and need somewhere to turn than it is when the world seems right.

I also consider these days of being pregnant as a memorial to our son if he doesn't make it. I won't take away this time or rush through it because, for now, he's hearing my voice, his heart beats inside me safely, and he must know the love I feel for him. It runs through my veins and every fiber of my being.

For this reason, I am convinced I would have more babies with Dylan if we had the opportunity. Time will tell. I'm trusting God to provide us with all we need and believing fully in that.

"While I'm fighting to believe,
I'm caught up in a battle I wasn't
looking for. You silence my worry
when fear is deafening. I think I
want answers, but what I really need
is peace."

- J. J. Heller

CHAPTER 20

Six Weeks Left and Counting Down

My pregnancy experience differed from everyone else I knew who was pregnant at the same time. I was the only one facing a high risk of losing my son from the very beginning. Because of this, I had to carve out my own way of moving through that time. In addition to declining a baby shower, I also had to decide if I wanted maternity photos. The trials of this pregnancy taught me about the importance of going against the standards and traditions that people hold so tightly if it protects your health – mental, physical, or spiritual – that supersedes the importance of doing things like everyone else.

Similar to the first year, the next generation takes over cooking for the holidays when Grandma can't anymore, and new traditions form. Sometimes, those traditions look like ordering a pizza so you don't burn down the house. There's no one way to do life, and I find a certain beauty in that thought.

In the end, I know I'll be able to look back on this time without regret because I was true to myself and honored my experience. I valued who I had to be at that time during those circumstances the way everyone should. I believed I would not always rely on the barrage of defense mechanisms built up during this pregnancy and was looking forward to who I would be when I had the chance to take a breath and relax again. With surgery to recover from and a newborn on the way, I realize it will likely be a long-awaited breath, but I'm looking forward to it anyway.

April 9th, 2020

On Monday evening, there was a tragic accident resulting in the passing of someone close to Dylan. He called me while I was sitting in my car in the parking lot of a greenhouse to tell me. The blood in my veins ran cold at his news, and the brightness of the sun shining through the car blinded my eyes. I was shocked and speechless with the latest news of another loss in our lives. It felt too close to the last loss we had that felt too close to the loss before that. I immediately thought of all those hurting for this person — so many loved ones surrounding this sweet soul who left us too soon.

Life makes no sense to me in times like these. I don't understand why some, like his friend, live to be fifty-one and others live to be one hundred.

I was only ten when I lost my grandfather. At the time, he was my best friend. Each loss after his always brought my mind back to him. He was the first person I grieved, and what can a ten-year-old teach you about loss anyway? I still haven't got the hang of it fifteen years later. I said a prayer for the family and asked God if he could join the rest of our family in heaven to watch over us.

Dylan goes through so much and remains strong. I pray our son inherits that strength. These past few years have been heavy for us.

My dear friend who miscarried had the D&C procedure done yesterday. I wish there was a way to take even a fraction of her pain away. I have never prayed this much in my life for hope during such trials. I wish I could be present with her in person, but the pandemic removed that option for me.

The results of my thirty-four-week BPP scan are good. We needed some good news.

April 9th, 2020

The liver and intestines in his Omphalocele sac haven't changed much, which is great. Our son seems so happy tucked in there, and I'm so happy we still have him among all the loss surrounding us.

The schools are all closed until August which would be the next school year. I miss the children. They always make me smile. Life looks unfamiliar these days.

My sleep lately has been poor, but I have an appointment to see my chiropractor tomorrow. I'm hoping the adjustments will help me get some sleep. It's no wonder, with the stress, worry, isolation, and difficulties lately, that anyone is sleeping.

I don't have much time to process my feelings about the waves and waves of trouble, so I focus first on my mental health. I'm spacing out my workload so that the long list of what I have to do doesn't overwhelm me. When I finish the day's work, I usually need a nap. Daytime naps seem to work best because of how hard it is for me to sleep through the night. It's good practice for the sleep I'll be getting (or not getting) once the little man arrives. He's growing quickly now. It's unbelievable to think how close we are to the finish line or the starting line, depending on how you frame it.

My niece, Evie, is seven months old. She is the bright spot in my world. I would lay down my life for her. Same with this baby in my belly.

I'm practicing gratitude when I can, but mostly, I'm grateful for Dylan and his strength. My next appointment in Pittsburgh is in thirty-three days.

April 21st, 2020

It's been almost two weeks since I had the chance to process my thoughts. I've been learning to meditate. It is fun for me and a great tool to help me relax my mind. I've done it about four times now. It's pure gold to me!

I look forward to going to our room, closing the room-darkening blinds, and laying there with the hypnotist on speakerphone as she guides me through the process. She helps me visualize the positive and focus on the good. It's been amazing. I can't wait to utilize this in the delivery room. I picture myself on the hill overlooking our town. I am strong, confident, and walking with ease. I am with my grandma — birds are singing all around us. I breathe easy as Grandma sends me loving vibes. The protection of Mother Mary surrounds us both. This is my happy place. It is sunny outside, and I feel warm in this vision. I envision my son there with me, too. It has taken me a long time to get these images to stick, and I am learning so much about myself in the process.

I am eating more protein-rich foods and noticing my sleep is improving. Shocking! The pandemic hasn't let up, so my prayers haven't either. One day, looking back on this time, it will be interesting to see what the pandemic has changed. It is so very overwhelming for everyone.

Dylan and I are single-handedly keeping our local Dairy Queen in business. God, I love ice cream!

On the seventeenth, I had a fantastic doctor's appointment in Pittsburgh. My mom was able to drive me there, though I had to go in alone. We shed some tears and laughed in the car, though, which made the trip memorable.

April 21st, 2020

Our son weighs five pounds and six ounces and is measuring in the twentieth percentile. His Omphalocele sac no longer has intestines in it, just his liver, although that could change. It measures six centimeters in size. This made everyone in the room happy. In twenty-three days, I will meet the second love of my life.

Yesterday was a great day. I felt really good. Today, I feel sore, almost crampy. My left sciatic nerve is angry and pinched. I'm still riding the waves of this life, feeling less caught in the undertow and more like my head remains above water.

I must be feeling incredibly positive because I changed my earlier decision not to have a maternity shoot.

Our wedding photographer, Kelsee, worked out a way to have a virtual photo shoot. I'm so happy about it. After all the time I spent journaling every moment of this pregnancy, I realized it would be a tragedy not to have photographic proof. I want Kelsee to capture the joy I feel. She was able to turn my ideas into reality somehow because of her creativity. I want us to be able to provide hope to others who may be pregnant and scared during this pandemic. The pictures will also be a surprise for our parents. Our moms specifically have had to deal with this pregnancy being more about survival than celebration, and I'd like to give them some of their joy back. We want to celebrate all that there is to celebrate as a way of taking back our power from all that tried to rob us of it.

To get in a mindset of enjoying the remaining weeks of this pregnancy, I plan on praying and meditating daily. I'm going to be intentional about making my love for Dylan apparent every day. The countdown is on.

April 23rd, 2020

We decided to take impromptu maternity pictures, and it was a genuinely great experience. I owe Kelsee Forsythe a big thanks for capturing both my wedding and my pregnancy so well. She was able to work her magic behind the scenes from the safety of her own home while capturing memories for me I never thought I'd get. I'm so grateful to have these pictures as a reminder to cherish this season of my life. Dylan and I wore blue. She graciously dropped off some outfits for me to choose from and wear.

Kelsee was able to do this for us via Facetime. She called us, then blocked the image of herself taking the pictures with greenery and snapped the pictures from her phone while guiding us on how to pose. I felt beautiful and loved the way my hair and makeup came out (that I spent hours working on). I was proud that I was finally gaining weight and proud to be carrying a little fighter. I felt so humbled to be his mom.

The baby was kicking the entire time. I always want to remember how much it seemed like he wanted to make sure he was a part of the photos and memories, too. As for me, well I am not sure how I stopped myself from crying during it all. I was so very emotional. I felt so blessed. My favorite picture is the one she took of his already-packed suitcase full of books I wanted to read to him and outfits I hoped to see him wear.

Kelsee posted some of the pictures online, which gave us the first opportunity to announce our high-risk pregnancy publicly. We didn't plan on making a post on Facebook to prevent any messages asking for more details and to protect our peace overall. We were pleasantly surprised when many more people saw the post than those in our usual circle of friends and families. There was an outpouring of love and support.

April 23rd, 2020

I received message after message with stories of other incredible people from people who faced similar issues during their pregnancies.

JJ Heller has a song called "Missing Peace" that was sent to me by a dear friend after she saw our post. As I listened to the music, I lost it, bawling over the dish of lasagna I was making. The song was so relatable it gave me chills. I had a good cry over how hard the battle was — the mental struggles the worst of all. I'm grateful some resources shed light on the mental toll of high-risk pregnancies. The lyrics are as follows:

I know it's here somewhere, the faith I used to have.

Before the sky fell down on me behind the curtain,

beneath the hospital bed, hiding just beyond my reach.

Feels like my prayers are bouncing off the ceiling tiles like a helium balloon.

I can't close the distance between the way I feel and what I know is true.

I'm caught up in a battle I wasn't looking for.

When I'm searching for solace in the middle of a war.

You are, you are my missing peace.

I'm tired of waiting, but I'm afraid of how it's gonna end,

so I'm stuck here in between bracing for bad news and hoping for a miracle.

While I'm fighting to believe, I'm caught up in a battle I wasn't looking for.

You silence my worry when fear is deafening.

I think I want answers, but what I really need is peace.5

April 23rd, 2020

I hold on to the fact that this baby is such a little beast. He passed another BPP examination today. I'm lucky to have access to these, and I'm grateful Nicole, my favorite ultrasound technician, was there today. She is amazing. I'm looking forward to introducing our son to her someday soon. He was sucking his thumb during the scans. I will not be the type of mom who gets mad at thumb-sucking; he is just providing himself comfort. I feel lucky to have made it to thirty-six weeks — even through my tears, I know how lucky I am.

It's been an emotional day going through messages and comments online. I look forward to when Dylan gets home. He is my best friend. As I am writing in my journal, I can hear the wind chimes and see the cardinals outside my windows. Cardinals are often thought of as our loved ones returning to give us their well-wishes. They are a good omen. After seeing them, my anxiety calmed a bit, and I was able to breathe and think more clearly.

I know the next twenty-one days will fly by. I'm ready to meet our son and to be a mom. I remember trying to envision myself as a wife before Dylan and I were married. No concrete images came to mind except getting to kiss and hold Dylan every day. Now here I am in the same situation, unable to imagine a concrete image of being with our son except to hold him. His way of loving me is what made it possible for me to give more love to our son. I love the life we are building together. Seeing him with our niece Evelynn reminds me of how wonderful he will be to our son.

I feel loved, prayed for, and supported more than ever today.

"Because of you I can feel myself slowly but surely becoming the me I have always dreamed of being."

- Tyler Knott Gregson

CHAPTER 21

Making It To the Finish Line

April 27th, 2020

We are getting Nan and Pa's old car. It is more of a family car than the one we have now. We are likely going to be moving soon as well. I'm looking forward to the move despite the work it will take to make it our own. At the end of the day, the house will have more space and we'll have a yard. I am always trying to look ahead to this baby thriving and our future family needing space like a bigger house and yard.

The next chapter of our lives will be having the baby. I thought my water broke yesterday, but it was a false alarm. It was a terrifying experience. Being a first-time mom is daunting. It's one first after another — each experience gained from something you've never been through before. My psyche was negatively affected, but Dylan was calm and cute about it. He was loving toward me as we drove to the maternity ward. He seemed so much more prepared for whatever we faced than I was. They sent me home with the diagnosis of Braxton Hicks contractions.

We are only seventeen days away from the delivery date. I'll be thirty-nine weeks and one day when we go in for the C-section on May 14th. Lately, my mind wanders to a chromosomal cause of our son's Omphalocele. Thankfully, my friends helped me to process those thoughts. Part of the reason I write all my thoughts down is so our son can see all the ways he is loved and supported through the people in our lives he hasn't met yet; there are so many people rooting for him and us.

I'm once again proud of myself and Dylan for how far we made it. We have already put in the work of taking this parenting thing seriously. Our son is loved, and that love looks like work, perseverance, and resilience.

April 27th, 2020

I'm so thankful for our family and friends. Maybe it's their outpouring of support or the daily prayers, devotions, and meditation, but I've found myself lately feeling content with whatever the outcome of this. I know God's will will be done, and I find it easy to believe that the best result is possible. Even as a person who needs to feel in control, it feels good to let some of that go and to trust. I trust in the love by our sides to get us through whatever the next few weeks look like. I continue to tell our son how big, brave, and strong he is. I continue to remind Dylan how amazing he's been through it all. I continue to meditate on empowering thoughts — that I can do this, that I am capable. Until May fourteenth comes along, I will stay as calm as I can in order to become the newest version of myself: a mother.

May 4th, 2020

Today, the baby weighed six pounds. He was a feisty one at the appointment! He wouldn't stop moving! I've made it to thirty-seven weeks and five days. I'm a statistical anomaly because most Omphalocele babies are often premature. I'll take the win. I can't wait to see him in person. We are hoping to make it just ten more days. It's all on his timing, though, I know. Then, we will finally get to meet the missing piece of our very own puzzle.

Dylan was informed that he will have paid time off while we have the baby, and the rest of the time he's off, they are permitting him to work from the hospital. He is back working full-time now with COVID precautions. Speaking of COVID-19, it's still wreaking havoc on the world, but Dylan is allowed to be with me and the baby during delivery.

May 4th, 2020

I'm absolutely thrilled and thankful for that news! It almost makes it okay that I have to have a C-section. Maybe I'm feeling overconfident now. This kid is a trooper! God is so good — always.

Whatever road leads me to my son is a good one for me.

May 13th, 2020

There have been many new developments since May 4th. We went to DuBois Hospital on the sixth due to contractions that wouldn't stop after my chiropractor appointment. They continued through dinner with my sister and an online appointment with my OBGYN. They lasted almost three hours, from 9 p.m. until 12 a.m.

Finally, at the hospital, three different people tried to check my cervix. It was awful. Dylan held my hand during it as I bawled. I was not dilated or in active labor, and they were able to discharge me home that night, but I had another BPP with an ultrasound the next day. Our son was not as active as they would have liked, so they used a device to "zap" my belly, causing it to vibrate to see if he would respond. I was still having active contractions every five to six minutes. The baby's BPP score was an 8. We went home first against medical advice because we wanted to grab our hospital bag and drive to Pittsburgh. They preferred to fly me there.

We did make it to Pittsburgh, and they placed an IV to get me hydrated. I was dilated one centimeter and 50% effaced. Because of this, they told me we could have the baby that night at 8 p.m., but I decided not to. I wanted to give him as much time as I could.

May 13th, 2020

Our parents met us in Pittsburgh and stayed in an Airbnb owned by my good friend Nicole's brother. It was only two miles away from the hospital where I would be delivering. The doctors cleared us to wait until Monday to have the baby as long as I promised to remain close by. They were relieved when they learned I would be staying a few miles away, not returning home about 2 hours away. This just happened to be over Mother's Day weekend. I got to spend my very first Mother's Day on the couch with my mother before becoming a mother myself. I was grateful for that time and that the baby was okay through all the scares.

Dylan's mom and sister, Alexis, made their way to see us as well.

Monday came quickly, and I went in for another ultrasound. Dylan and I decided together to have the baby after the ultrasound. After being in labor for several days, I wanted to be done. I gave everything I had to get our son to the goal of thirty-nine weeks and one day, but I didn't have anything left to give.

Remember earlier when I mentioned that our original maternal-fetal medicine physician was moving from my small town to Pittsburgh? She happened to be there and handled our care on that Monday before delivering our son. She reviewed my ultrasound images and came in to discuss them just as she did on November 13th when we got the news of his Omphalocele. I am convinced this was not a coincidence. Her opinion mattered to me because we built up trust when I was seeing her in Dubois.

I discussed my wish to deliver that very day, as handling the contractions was not fun. She urged me to try and make it to Thursday. Thursday would be the original planned 39-week and one-day date.

May 13th, 2020

She believed I was capable of this, so I continued the next few days while experiencing intermittent contractions. Because of her support and the trust we built, I decided to push through. I knew she supported the best possible outcome for both me and our son, so I wanted to be strong. She gave me more strength than I thought I had.

I'm not sure how my body held out for those additional days, but now we are just fourteen short hours away from meeting our son. I am so grateful my parents came down to be with us for those days bunkered down in what felt like a ghost town during the pandemic. We ordered in food, needing to be curbside picked up, and walked down the bare, people-less streets, that once were busy and booming. They were with me during such an unknown time, both pregnancy-wise and pandemic-wise. Everyone talks about the infant stage as the one when you need your parents the most, but I needed them there at that moment to get through those days, leading to becoming a parent myself.

Dylan and I got a hotel directly behind the hospital and will stay there until the morning with my parents as well. I am experiencing a new feeling I can only describe as eager but terrified.

Tomorrow, we will become parents. I can't believe we made it. We freaking made it!

"I have far more to learn from you than you could ever learn from me."

- Lauren Grant

CHAPTER 22

A Brief Encounter With the Second Love of My Life

May 14th, 2020

The day we met our son, I wouldn't allow myself the excitement of what was about to happen. I woke up nervous, uncertain, and excited. In my anxiety, I texted Dylan's best man, asking him to take care of Dylan if something happened to me. As I hugged my parents goodbye before leaving for the hospital, I felt more of an adult than ever. It was surreal.

At the hospital, the nurses wheeled me to the operating room without Dylan for my epidural placement. I was a child again, more afraid than I ever was. The doctors were concerned my blood pressure was too low. There was a possibility that they would need to perform a classical C-section as well. This procedure would require them to cut my uterus vertically to ensure our son could be removed without rupturing the Omphalocele. I consented to it, and it was decided that it was necessary.

I listened to their concerns and all the warnings, but about three minutes into their spiel, my eyes rolled back in my head. In the words of the operating room staff, I began to tank. The anesthesiologist was at the head of the bed with me, walking me through deep breathing. He told me that I needed to let him know how I was feeling, and I was able to express feeling very dizzy, light-headed, extremely cold, and a smidge nauseous. He explained to me how common it is that during a C-Section, the patient's blood pressure is not stable. He also told me my cesarean would be one of about fifteen that day. We made small talk, and it helped me keep my eyes open and gave me something other than my circumstances to think about.

May 14th, 2020

My face was flushed, my legs weren't fully numb, and my arms were heavy. My blood pressure began to rise but was still not at a level they felt was comfortable for Dylan to join us in the operating room. I had to receive a med to bring my blood pressure up, and finally, after what felt like an hour passed, the doctor told me it was taking effect.

I wasn't in a position to pretend I could do this alone and wasn't at ease until Dylan showed up at the head of my bed. He had on green scrubs in the loveliest shade. I remember he kept telling me to keep my eyes open and focus on him. The doctor encouraged me to remain calm, and he let me know I was doing a great job. I had my partner — together, we were about to meet our son.

I was cold, anxious, and groggy. I remember shivering the entire time I was in the operating room. Even though I couldn't feel the pain of the operation, there was an immense amount of pressure and pulling on my abdomen and surrounding areas. The drape that kept me from seeing the gory details of what was unfolding was a saving grace.

The room was full of strangers. Finally, they lowered the drape so we could see our son. At that moment, I never saw a more beautiful sight. He was perfect.

His color was terrific as the tiniest shriek echoed through the room — his first cry. He was here in the room with us. The stress over his Omphalocele for the greater half of the past year melted away. I don't even remember making a note of it when they showed us our son. It was everything to me to have our son in the room, living, breathing, alive, and he appeared well.

May 14th, 2020

I caught a glimpse of his Omphalocele and felt reassured that we could do this. I just knew this little boy had the strength to get through whatever came next. Seeing him was the first time I experienced the feeling that I would die for someone. More than that, I knew I could face anything ahead of us — for him. He was the reason Dylan and I met every obstacle in this pregnancy journey. The room of providers exclaimed a happy birthday to our son. It was 10:01 a.m. exactly.

As quickly as he arrived, our son was whisked away for his birth assessment. The room was eerily silent. Dylan was beside me, asking me to look him in the eyes. His presence was such a comfort to me. I locked my eyes with his and could feel the mutual sense of accomplishment between them. We did it. Two became three.

Our son scored an eight at his one-minute Apgar assessment and an eight again at five minutes. He needed some oxygen but was doing well. We weren't able to see him or touch him, but they did allow us to wave goodbye to him before they took him to the NICU to continue assessing him.

Even though the C-section caused pressure while it was performed, after the procedure, I felt like I could finally breathe. My body was numb. I was numb. I just wanted to be with our son, to hold him, sing to him, and watch those deep blue eyes respond to my voice. I wanted to call him by the name we gave him — Lincoln Andrew — over and over.

Dylan and I hugged for a long time after they took Lincoln. We talked about how he didn't look like either of us — just like this little wrinkly stranger.

May 14th, 2020

The end of my pregnancy was only the beginning of Lincoln's story. The neonatologist came into our room to let us know Lincoln required oxygen support for a brief time. He weighed 7 pounds, 11 ounces and measured 19.25 inches long. The positive news was music to my ears. They wheeled him to the post-operative room in his incubator, and we only got to hold his hand. They told us we could have a little over two minutes with him. The world stopped while we soaked in him. I thanked all the nurses and staff, along with God, and prayed for time to stop for a bit so we could bask in our son.

He was calm and content. I told him more than ten times how much love surrounded him. It stretched from our weary hearts in the room to our parents, our extended family, the nurses, the friends, all the way to the heavens. Its presence was in the hundreds of prayers and the guidance of the grandparents who were with us in spirit.

When he had to leave, it was the most painful goodbye. I was figuratively and literally empty without him. They transferred Lincoln to a hospital fifteen minutes away from us. It wasn't Dylan and I, his mom and dad, but strangers who shared my son's first road trip.

His absence from my side felt like a phantom limb. I wasn't able to kiss him, breathe in his scent, give him love, feed him, or embrace him. Two minutes of touching his tiny fingers as they wrapped around mine was not enough. No amount of explanations for what could happen prepared us for when it actually did.

Many parents take the first hour of their newborn's life to spend alone with them. It's affectionately called the golden hour. I felt robbed of that experience.

May 14th, 2020

My nursing background helped me understand why they took him, but there was no convincing the heart of a new mother. I longed for the day that Dylan, Lincoln, and I would be able to be together.

Shortly after they took Lincoln to the children's hospital, Dylan left to join him and make sure he wasn't alone. It was challenging to let him go, too, but he was also the only connection to our son until I was healed and cleared to join them. He told me he would relay all the info and updates on Lincoln. We all had long days ahead of us.

I sat for a moment, collecting my thoughts while I waited for my mom to arrive. I prayed for Dylan not to feel alone through the next few days. I felt small, like my job of getting him here was done, and there was nothing left to do when they took him.

After making it through the maze of COVID-related questions, hospital security, and the locked double doors guarding the maternity ward, my mother made it to me. An overwhelming amount of guilt came over me as I realized how much strength motherhood required. I felt terrible for any time I didn't recognize that or took it for granted in her. I was beginning to understand all the sacrifices she made and continued to make just by being there that day.

There are many books on parenting, but none I know of that talk about how to parent your adult children. There are some days you need your mother. I needed her that day and in the days that followed, and there she was.

May 16th, 2020

The experience I had after Lincoln's birth was a blur. I will never forget the sense of loss I felt from missing him and Dylan. The pain was nightmarish. My pride wouldn't let me take any painkillers until I was almost beyond its help.

My mother had the patience of a saint. She let me cry and confess every emotion through the spectrum of sadness I was experiencing and just listened. In quiet moments, she reminded me I would hold my son sooner than it felt. She gently reminded me I needed to put work into my recovery to get there. She helped me walk the halls, which was a crucial part of my recovery.

I was walking just hours after having my C-section. These regular walks were my way of getting to Lincoln as soon as I could. My mom always took them with me. She straightened my hair to give me some semblance of dignity and normalcy. We had many good talks about all that went on leading up to delivering Lincoln, how it went in the operating room, and how I felt without him or Dylan being a brand-new mom.

The two days apart from my boys went fast and slow at the same time. I pumped every few hours to get my supply up for our son. I was uncertain I'd be able to produce milk at all due to having a breast reduction at age nineteen. I was impressed my body was able to produce milk for Lincoln. Maybe it was the feeling that I did have a job and could contribute that made me want to continue breastfeeding him as long as my body cooperated. Dylan made the drive over just to collect the breast milk from my mom in the parking lot. Until I could produce enough, we also used donated breast milk to supplement.

May 16th, 2020

Dylan remained beside Lincoln while my mom and I watched them on the NICU camera from my hospital bed. It was surreal to watch stranger after stranger enter Lincoln's room to care for him and for me not to be there.

Because of the COVID restrictions and Lincoln's medical issues, none of our family could join us in celebrating Lincoln's birth until he was strong enough and likely discharged. My mother and I weren't the only ones who relied on video chatting and phone calls.

He required multiple specialists and providers so the healthcare workers were in the room consistently. Meanwhile, I was doing everything to heal so that I could reunite with them.

Two short days after delivering my son and after a gloriously refreshing shower, I was discharged to join my husband and son.

I hugged my mom for the longest time, knowing how much she was there for me the past couple of days and that I wouldn't get to see her for an indeterminate amount of time due to the pandemic. She was amazing, loving, and supportive during our time together in the hospital. She pushed me to pump, to walk, to heal, to process my emotions — all so that I could be as present as possible when it was my time to fill my maternal role. She was more than my mother; she was the lifeline I needed. I wouldn't have made it without her.

"What is done in love, is done well."

- Vincent Van Gogh

CHAPTER 23

From Husband to Father and Mother to Mother

I asked my mom and Dylan to share their thoughts on my pregnancy and their points of view:

Mom

When Shelbi and Dylan told me they were pregnant, all I could do was laugh. I was thrilled for them. Her dad and I had just welcomed our first grandchild weeks before she informed us that our second grandchild was on the way. My mind went to planning another baby shower and all the exciting milestones she had to look forward to. I also knew Shelbi as a daughter of "whys." She always examined every aspect of her circumstances to ensure she made the best possible decisions. I hoped and prayed with all my being that her pregnancy would be perfect for her. I knew she and Dylan would be excellent parents, and I was eager to support them through the day of their baby's birth.

Shelbi had her first sonogram and afterward came to our house with Dylan to share the results with her siblings and us. When she explained the diagnosis to us, I kept telling myself to stay calm and breathe. Every instinct in me wanted to cry, but I resolved to be strong for them.

Maybe I went through the steps of grief myself because, at first, it didn't feel real, then I was mad, and then I kept trying to convince myself that the doctors missed something – that somehow they were wrong.

As a mother, when something happens to your child, all you want to do is help, make it stop, and fix it, but I couldn't fix this. All I could do was offer to help. I wasn't sure exactly what that looked like, but I knew I wanted to try. Something happened, though, at each appointment, sonogram, and all the long months of her pregnancy: I started to recognize this strong person emerging. Shelbi handled it better than I thought she would. While it was hard for me to see that she missed out on the joy of that first pregnancy, I watched her redefine joy through and because of it.

When Shelbi told me she wanted me at the hospital with her so that Dylan could be with Lincoln, I was honored to do that for her. Shelbi only got to see Lin-

coln for a short time after delivery. Now, it was my job to take care of her.

I admit that all I wanted to do was cry again because she just gave birth. Her body and spirit were broken from being separated from her husband and son. So now our new joy was watching Lincoln on the baby cam and the videos Dylan sent us. We walked the halls and saw other newborns with their mothers there. I felt upset, like Shelbi was missing out on the experience of holding her son but then realized she wasn't. For the most part, she delivered the most beautiful and healthy baby boy. The accomplishment of that was astounding. I knew she would get to see him soon.

Once she was released, Shelbi went to her son and husband, and for the next several weeks, we only saw videos and pictures of Lincoln. That was probably the most challenging time for us. When I finally got to meet Lincoln for the first time, all the trials we went through to get to that moment melted away. It all seemed normal now because he was just perfect.

Dylan

After arguably the longest morning of my life, my whole world had changed, but even at this point, I did not know by how much.

Shelbi's mom, Jenn, met me at the front door of Magees Hospital. After a quick congrats and letting her know that Shelbi was okay, I ran to the car to hurry over to Children's to be with Lincoln.

It's impossible to overstate how nervous I was. I don't remember the entire car ride to the hospital except that I made a mental note to eat to have the energy to face the long days ahead.

I knew our lives would change drastically, but nothing could have prepared me for how much. I felt compelled to be Lincoln's supporter, advocate, and father.

Because of COVID restrictions, I would be alone for several days.

My fears came to a head when I walked into the room where Lincoln was. I went from scared to petrified. I remember the room seemed to have twenty people in it.

Someone on staff noticed me and said, "Hey, here's dad!" Everyone took a step back so I could get to him. I stood beside him for the first time. There were no barriers between him and me.

It isn't easy to describe what it was like seeing Lincoln up close and personal the first time. I saw many pictures of him inside the womb, but to see the pinkish-red wrinkled skin on his wrists and how his peaceful, tiny chest moved up and down with his breaths made him more real to me. Considering how much time we spent preparing for all the possibilities, I barely noticed the Omphalocele. It's not that I thought it wasn't important or ignored, but it seemed to make up more of his identity inside his mother than it did outside.

Linc, as I call him now, was calm and seemed much like any other newborn. Because he was calm, it had a soothing effect on me. At that point, I had an overwhelming feeling that everything would be okay.

I stared and smiled at him for what seemed like an hour. In all reality, it may have only been a few minutes, but afterward, I stepped back to let the doctors and nurses continue his work-up.

I sat in the room and took it all in.

I texted Shelbi to let her know I was with our son and would send a video soon. I knew it would make her so happy to see him even though her heart was breaking to be separated from us.

After finding the coffee vending machine, I walked back to the room. I wanted to be vigilant, but I was fading around three in the morning. I started playing music quietly on my phone to help me stay awake and noticed that Lincoln started crying when I played Luke Comb's cover of "Fast Car." To this day, he still tells me to change that song when it comes on.

The next day and a half are hard to put into words. Many emotions were vying for the front of my thoughts. I was proud to be Linc's father and to be by his side to see all the firsts he had. I collected those minor moments like they were priceless gold, from his first stretch after waking up from a nap to the first time a nurse fed him from a syringe. At the same time, I was sad because my wife – my partner in life and my soul mate – wasn't there by my side. Those days without her were painful to me. We FaceTimed each other every chance we had. The hospital even provided a baby NICU camera for his hospital room so that she had access to watch him 24/7, but it wasn't the same.

Shelbi's 48-hour cesarean recovery period was over, and she was finally discharged and on the way to Lincoln's hospital. I watched her see him for the first time and hold him. That was my favorite first to witness of them all.

The circumstances of the past nine months weighed heavily on our relationship, but seeing our son and watching each other become his parents brought us closer than we ever were before. We learned how to fight for each other by fighting for Lincoln. We learned a new side of each other by witnessing the beautiful new creation of ourselves as parents. We learned to savor the good by understanding that the bad could only take away so much. We learned to appreciate each moment instead of striving for more. We learned to work on what we could control by being thrown into a situation we could not.

The hospital staff of doctors and nurses were there at a moment's notice, but ultimately, we knew it was up to us from here to figure out what he needed.

Feeding Lincoln was a more significant obstacle than I like to admit. Neither Shelbi nor I looked forward to it. He almost always had trouble keeping it down. It seemed by the time you warmed the bottle, fed him, burped him, cleaned all of the bottling equipment, and sat back down (praying he would not throw it back up), it would be time to feed him again. One of the things we struggled with was time management as we got used to this new system. Like all life changes, we learned to adjust and make the most of it.

Wedged right in the middle of our new life, Shelbi and I had some great moments that I look back on fondly. We sometimes had mini lunch "dates" to the hospital cafeteria. Shelbi took my discovery of the coffee vending machine near our room to the next level when she found out there was a Starbucks in the hospital. Confidently, I can say it was a much better alternative to the vending machine coffee.

I am acutely aware that Lincoln had a different birth story than many babies, but looking back, I wouldn't change it for anything. The scar on his stomach and his fake belly button is part of what makes Lincoln who he is, and they point to the story we share as a family. His birth marked the beginning of the three of us — the laughs, scares, snuggly naps, sleepless nights, all the way to our present story.

I remember those nights at the hospital with Shelbi. We figured out that the couch was the most comfortable place to sleep side by side together. We didn't mind how small and cramped it was. The trundle bed was even smaller. At that time in our lives, we needed each other's closeness. We held on to each other both literally and figuratively through every moment, terrible and wonderful.

May 17th, 2020

When I got to the hospital and made it to Lincoln's room, my fear disappeared. I was in a flood of emotions the first time I held my son. We lived in a vortex where time didn't exist. I questioned everything during my pregnancy, but having him was the answer I was looking for the entire time. He was a trophy at the finish line of all my fears.

I soaked in the feeling of being in the NICU room and took my time trying to capture every image I could to remember that moment and feeling — Lincoln's mom. I was Lincoln's mom, the one who fought daily battles to reach this moment. An army of people prayed for this moment. I begged for it for almost two years. The feeling of holding him got me through the worst days of my life. The moment I imagined was happening in real life.

My son got to feel the love of being in my arms. He got to hear the sound of love in my voice. I got to connect with him the way I desperately wanted to from the beginning of his life. What difference does a two-day delay make after what felt like a lifetime of waiting? We had him.

I took my time studying Lincoln's features and captured every memory I could. He was a lanky baby. His Omphalocele was wrapped, and his body was currently tubeless. His clipped fingernails were still a little scratchy, and his toes were long. I examined the hints of his personality shining through in his movements. He smelled like a newborn on the beach, swaddled in the hospital blankets.

He was here, earthside. As I held him, I had no idea how I would ever let him go. I also knew that if it ever came to it, I would lay down my life for him — I'd sacrifice anything to see him happy and thriving.

May 17th, 2020

I was grateful that Dylan didn't leave his side while I couldn't be there. Watching him hold our son for the first time multiplied my love for him. I'm so grateful we have a picture of it.

We were grateful to have our boy with us, but a new set of fears replaced those I experienced while carrying him. The staff at the children's hospital informed us he had ASD, or an atrial septal defect, which means he had a hole in his heart. He also had hydronephrosis, which is a kidney issue that prevents him from flushing excess fluids and urine.

Dylan and I were awaiting the lab results of the genetic panel. Those results would take nearly eight weeks to arrive. I was emotional and tired after meeting doctor after doctor to discuss Lincoln's care. Truthfully, I felt a pang of jealousy when meeting medical staff who had more interactions with our son than I did. It was like they knew more about our son than us. I was emotional and jealous during those days, feeling like the moments we had with him in between his care were never enough. On top of that, I was still healing from my C-section, tending to the large wound under my abdominal wall, and still had pain medication coursing through my veins.

I was less prepared for the ordinary aspects of newborns. He was just like a normal baby, just with a little extra going on. He was a star patient the first week. By the seventh day, he graduated from the NICU to a step-down unit. It was a relief after seven sleepless nights, so many tears, puke, and diaper changes, all the late-night care plans made with the medical team, and the daily rounds of seeing specialist after specialist to move on to the next phase of his care. We had a long road ahead of us still and were happy to move forward.

"There are places in the heart you don't even know exist until you love a child"

- Anne Lamott

CHAPTER 24

God Bless the NICU Nurses

The neonatal intensive care unit, or NICU, is the safest place for your infant to be when they have medical issues but the scariest place as a parent. I felt the pain of the other parents who had to watch their children fight to survive in their first days and for the children who fought.

Each morning, Dylan and I would grab a coffee to get time just the two of us. I recall glancing into a few other rooms on the NICU floor. One new mother was holding her infant in one hand. She was a micro premie and the smallest infant I ever saw. In another room, there were balloons and gifts for a child celebrating their first birthday. They were in the hospital for their entire first year. It was unfathomable to me. There were twins in the room beside us. We watched their parents visit daily before and after work.

I want to take a moment to acknowledge the nurses who deal with these harrowing circumstances every day, all while making the experience less traumatic and terrifying for those going through it. Our nurses, Nicole C. and Kirsten C., were among those who made our time in the hospital stay the best experience it could be. They advocated for Lincoln and kept us involved in every step of his care. They treated us with dignity and genuinely loved our sweet son. I was most grateful for their presence at his side when Dylan and I couldn't be there. I intend to stay in touch with them and give them updates on Lincoln as he continues to grow.

It was our seventh day in the NICU, and I wanted to order sushi for lunch. We took it to the parent cafe on the floor, and while I ate, I couldn't stop crying. For the seven days of Lincoln's life, I held my composure so that I could attend to his needs. That day, it became too much. Another NICU mom kept glancing at me from her table. She asked Dylan if I was okay, and he shook his head yes. Not long after, she moved beside me to offer comfort. She asked me how long we were there. I told her, "Today is a week." She explained to me that her daughter had been in the NICU for seven months to the day. She shared some more details about what that was like. After our conversation, I regained some control over my emotions and gathered up my things to head back to our son. The conversation we had with that other mom made me feel less alone. She was able to walk with us for a small part of our journey with incredible consideration, even as she was in the middle of her struggle. It gave me a new perspective.

There is a camaraderie of being in the NICU between those going through that ordeal. We often passed the same parents in the hall or the cafe and began to bond over the shared circumstance. There are many reasons families require the care of the NICU. Primarily, its purpose is to give individualized care at the highest levels for the infants, as each child gets one nurse per shift. There are many family situations there as well. Some infants had to stay isolated to keep their immune systems safe. I was grateful that Dylan and I were able to be present with Lincoln for the duration of his stay. We had no intention of leaving his bedside until they discharged him. I like to think I matured about ten years in that week.

May 21st, 2020

Lincoln graduated from the NICU today. Of all the emotions I felt this past week, none was more surprising than the sense of familiarity we had with our room in wing 8B. It was the first place I got to hold Lincoln and the first place we settled into the new reality of being a family of three. I fed him in that room, read to him for the first time, and watched Dylan be a father for the first time as well. We even grew an attachment to the nurses who held me up during my weakest moments.

Dylan's care for me was more profound than I ever felt possible. He helped me shower and kept telling me it was going to be okay — we were going to be okay.

The step-down unit was on the sixth floor in bed 6A of room 632. This was our new home away from home.

I FaceTimed our parents to give them an update and show them the view. This room was where I could watch the sun rise and set, day after day, until we could bring our tiny bundle of sunshine home. I had trouble getting my words out through the flood of emotions. I felt like I had defeated the big boss in a video game and that we were one step closer to conquering the hospital. I had to cut the FaceTime calls short so I could gather my emotions. In the evenings, I turned to the shower — it had become my thinking place, an emotional release safety net of sorts.

We were fortunate for the access the room gave us to Lincoln. The care of our son fell on Dylan and me. We now called the shots and were the first in line to make the decisions for his care. It was exciting and terrifying.

Lincoln's job was to keep going, and boy, was he a fighter. The strength I knew he had while inside me was proved each day that we had him.

May 21st, 2020

The surgical team came up with a plan for our son in that room, and we agreed. After Lincoln was discharged to our care at home, we would take over the intense wound care for his Omphalocele for four to six months. He would be a surgical candidate in one to two years. They were confident that his case would have a positive outcome.

I gained a sense of peace as I saw Lincoln progress through his care. We did physical therapy, occupational therapy, and speech therapy throughout our stay on the surgical floor. We learned how to modify tummy time, how to burp him to avoid reflux and help decrease risk of aspiration, and other ways to adapt his care around his needs. He was a typical newborn aside from his midsection.

Our most significant obstacle to taking him home was his weight. He puked after almost every feed, making it difficult for him to gain weight. We gradually increased his volume, learning the limits of his care. Lincoln set the pace of intake because he was the only one who felt the pressure in his belly from eating. We learned to take our time, and interestingly, he could sense my anxiety. I had to relax around him so that he could relax around me. We learned to trust each other in those early stages — his of life and mine of being a mother.

During that time, I fought to breastfeed him. The doctors gave me the green light to start when he was fourteen days old. This accomplishment came at the hands of several lactation consultants and speech therapists to help me get Lincoln in the best position for him and me. I continued to pump and feed to ensure my supply remained adequate. I prayed continually to be able to provide him with that type of nourishment.

May 21st, 2020

It was also a beautiful way to bond with our son and proved to the hospital staff that we had more than one way to feed him besides the bottle. I was able to pump so much breast milk for him leading up to his discharge that I had a robust stockpile to take home with us. I was in complete awe at the life we created and of my ability to provide nourishment for him.

They say that a new version of yourself is born the day your child is born, and every moment I had with him made that more of a reality.

Becoming a mother was scary, anxiety-filled, bittersweet, and beautiful. I gained confidence in tending to my care and our son's. I gained perspective from the circumstantial relationships I formed while here. I opened a new level of understanding of my husband as the caring father of our child. I found a new love for the softness of my body that is forever changed inside and out. I learned to pray through the sleepless nights — mostly prayers of gratitude. I learned more about grace, hope, and patience in those weeks than the years I spent in church. I felt the presence of God close beside me within those walls. It made me more of a fighter and believer.

Before discharge, one of the final steps before leaving the hospital was to have him circumcised. Thankfully, that procedure happened without any complications.

On the day of discharge, we got Lincoln a special car seat called the Hope Car Bed. He was strapped in with Velcro and laid horizontally in a plastic rectangle without a cover on it. It was far from ideal, but it was the only way we could get him home safely. We were grateful it was at least manageable for us.

May 21st, 2020

Looking back at the hospital doors as we were about to leave, I felt every memory from our time there at once. From asking hundreds of questions every day to the emotional breakdowns in the parent cafe to the words of encouragement and the sense of camaraderie with strangers to becoming lifelong friends with the countless nurses, care technologists, and doctors involved in our care — I witnessed miracle after miracle. The latest one belonged to us. We were taking our son home.

I knew life was about to get even more interesting.

"People think they know you. They think they know how you're handling a situation. But the truth is no one knows. No one knows what happens when you leave them when you're lying in bed or sitting over breakfast alone, and all you want to do is cry or scream. They don't know what's going on inside your head—the mind-numbing cocktail of anger, sadness, and guilt. This isn't their fault. They just don't know. And so they pretend, and they say you're doing great when really you're not. And this makes everyone feel better — everybody but you."

— William H. Woodwell Jr.

CHAPTER 25

Postpartum Anxiety and Depression

A quote by Donald Rumsfeld kept popping into my head the months after Lincoln was born: "You don't know what you don't know."

No amount of parenting books could prepare me for the months after Lincoln was born. I didn't know if my emotional response to each issue I encountered was normal or abnormal. I wasn't sure if my loved ones saw how badly I struggled or if I was hiding that side of myself as well as I hoped I had been. I didn't have the tools or experience to know what was okay to be thinking or feeling.

I've mentioned my history of depression and anxiety throughout this book. Before and during my pregnancy, I felt I had the support and tools to win against the attacks on my mental health. I was confident that my previous experiences were good enough to ensure I'd avoid postpartum depression and anxiety. In retrospect, I suspect I suffered from both.

A great deal of my efforts during my pregnancy went into trying to ensure Lincoln would make it to his delivery date. We had plans in place for his care after he was born, and then we were blindsided by COVID-19. No one could have predicted that plot twist!

There he was with us after months of every fear imaginable. But his birth was more a starting line than the finish. From there, the pressure to care for him increased, coinciding with a marked decrease in the quality and quantity of my sleep.

To start, there was pressure to make sure he was safe, growing, and free from sickness. We also had to monitor him for the potential risks that an Omphalocele brought on, such as constipation, chronic vomiting, and difficulty breathing that sometimes happens due to the extra pressure on his stomach and diaphragm. Every day, we had to clean and dress the wound to keep it from infection.

Our biggest issue was that he threw up almost every time we fed him. My anxiety came in waves. My need to control the situation as a way to comfort myself had me tracking the ounces of formula he drank and guessing how much weight he would lose each time he puked. I weighed his soiled and wet diapers and tracked those numbers. I created a folder in my cell phone where I kept records of how much he ate, how much I pumped, and how much his weight would fluctuate each day. I started to obsess over these numbers and worry about missing an aspect of his health that would delay or inhibit his care.

I probably shouldn't have tortured myself in this way, but I was a first-time mother with a medically complex infant on my hands. To say the territory I was navigating was new is an understatement.

I kept trudging through the postpartum trenches, every day feeling more overwhelmed and exhausted. I barely slept during that time – not just from having a newborn, but the fear that he would stop breathing paralyzed me. I was already waking every two to four hours to pump for the first two months, along with feeding him every two to four hours as well so I'd also take the time to make sure he was still alive. That was one of my biggest fears.

Many of the fears during my pregnancy were still haunting me. The fear I might lose the pregnancy was multiplied by the hundreds now that we had this perfect child we could see, hold, and cherish. He had a name and a personality; he was more ours than ever, and we couldn't fathom losing him.

As wonderful as it was to bring him home, we also left the care of an expert medical team. It was daunting as new parents to be on our own in the real world.

If any of my friends or family noticed my obsessive behavior, they never mentioned it to me. I'm sure it was noticeable. As a nurse, I felt competent taking care of him medically, but there was no distinct line between nurse and mother that you have when it's your patient. You get to clock out when it's a patient.

The other aspect of those months that I struggled with was feeling isolated. We couldn't go anywhere due to Lincoln's inability to ride in a car seat. A typical car seat was not safe due to the pressure it would place on his abdomen. The hospital-provided car seat was not one I was fond of and would never use without a passenger right beside Lincoln so we barely left home for months on end. Remember, we were already stuck inside due to the pandemic.

Hours ran into days, ran into weeks, ran into months. Initially, I didn't even know how to shower because I was too anxious to take my eyes off Lincoln.

Dylan returned to work after his leave was up, which left me more alone. We couldn't have many visitors because of the pandemic, but I also think there was a hesitance of some people on how to approach Lincoln's Omphalocele. I didn't hold that against anyone, but being by myself wore me down. I have always preferred being around other people. There were times I wondered if life would ever settle into a rhythm of normalcy and if I would ever sleep through the night again.

I wish I would have been more honest with myself about the toll motherhood took on me. A part of me felt guilty for struggling, considering that our son was the answer to many fervent prayers. I didn't want to need more help, but Lincoln and I both would have benefitted had I been brave enough to ask for it.

Any number of actions could have taken a massive burden off my shoulders had I realized the trouble I was having sooner. I should have reached out to a family member and explained I needed help. I could have enlisted the help of my OBGYN office for psychiatric referrals. Therapy or even anti-anxiety meds would have helped as well. I was battling two wars – the one I was fighting to keep Lincoln thriving and the other invisible battle against my mind.

I do want to take a moment to specify that I was asked multiple times by those who supported me how I was doing. Whether it was pride, foolishness, or my previous experiences with depression and anxiety, I felt it would eventually pass. Even though I was uncertain of when or how the struggle would pass, I kept thinking I could handle it, so I held onto it.

I admonish anyone reading this to do the opposite of what I did. If even one new mother can learn from my mistakes, then admitting them will be worth it. Physicians are there to help. Trust that when family or friends reach out with offers of support, it's because they genuinely want to help also.

Don't be afraid to admit if you are struggling or having dark thoughts. There are therapists, therapeutic solutions, and support groups. You aren't alone in struggling. Many new mothers feel postpartum depression and anxiety. These are especially prevalent in those who have a baby with medical issues.

I acknowledge now more than ever just how much mental health affects every aspect of your being, especially once you are a mother. Through therapy, I have learned and unlearned things. I like the good that I have gained, the bad that I have lost, and who I've become through my sessions.

The bottom line is your family needs you present and whole. Getting help or taking time to care for yourself is not selfish; it's essential.

"Carry on, brave mother. Carry on, brave mother who tries when she's tired. Carry on, brave mother who gives unconditionally. Carry on, brave mother who cries because she loves. Carry on, brave mother who hopes without answers. Carry on, brave mother who loves without expectations. Carry on, brave mother. Carry on."

— Rachel Marie Martin

CHAPTER 26

The Battle of Medical Setbacks and Triumphs

When you undergo a Cesarean delivery, your body has to recover from an intense surgery where seven layers of your skin and abdomen are cut along with your uterus. There is blood loss, fluid loss, and cauterization to stop the bleeding. Your core is left with adhesions and significant scars.

In my case, the C-section required my uterus to be cut vertically. The pain was immense, but I think my drive to see our son got me through it in record time.

Lincoln was my reason from the first moment we found out about his existence. He was my reason to advocate for his life and health, my motivation to seek support during my pregnancy, and my determination to persevere through my recovery. Because of him, I learned I was stronger than I thought. He continues to be my daily reason for becoming the best person and mother possible.

After we left the hospital, Dylan and I had to find an accessible pediatrician to take over Lincoln's care. The closest doctor willing to see him and also experienced with an Omphalocele was an hour's drive from us. For just shy of the first year of his life, we took that drive frequently.

Before he turned a year old, we found a physician fifteen minutes away. The local provider knew that if any issues came up, we would by-pass his office and head straight to Pittsburgh for his medical team.

In July, the year after Lincoln was born, he started throwing up what looked like coffee grounds. Thankfully, due to my medical background, I knew it was blood from somewhere, so we headed to the children's hospital. The timing was poor because Dylan's friends were throwing him a diaper party when I frantically called him to get us. Our local hospital doesn't have a pediatric floor, so we took the two-hour drive. My mom came with us even though she knew she wouldn't be allowed in the room with us – COVID was very much still restrictive when it came to healthcare. Only parents were allowed in with the child.

My concern was that Lincoln may have had bleeding in his intestines or a bowel obstruction. It was challenging to return to the hospital, but incredibly, we had some of the same nurses we befriended. They loved how remarkable his progress was and how much he had grown since we left.

I was less anxious this time around, but I felt the echoes of trauma from all that we experienced in that place. We had lived there for weeks. My chest felt heavy to return, but it was more important that Lincoln was okay.

They placed Lincoln on what's called bowel rest and didn't allow him to drink anything. After staying the night, we were discharged. The doctors ran tests and just thought it was a bad case of reflux. He continued to puke for the next handful of days, but the doctors eased my mind.

At home, it was a relief to be back in our comfort zone. My bed was heavenly, and Lincoln slept through the entire night, so he must have felt it too.

We qualified for home health nursing visits to check on his weight a few times per week. The nurse was lovely. She helped me gain more confidence in feeding and pumping, and she adored Lincoln. She had an upbeat personality that always put me at ease when she was around. Admittedly, it was nice to have someone else in the house. I was so grateful for her help and support during that time, so much so that she was one of the first people I sent a picture of Lincoln's belly to when his wound healed up around mid-August.

I was part-nurse and part-mother to Lincoln as well. Settling into a routine of checking his poop and vomit for changes or blood was the nurse in me. Making sure I loved him, touched him often, and spoke and sang to him was the mom in me.

Many Omphalocele kids are thinner and smaller than the average child. It was a constant source of concern that he was growing steadily, and it was also one of the most straightforward markers for us to track his progress.

His weight gain was gradual but consistent until around months nine to twelve of his life. During those three months, he only gained around two to three pounds. His doctor said he needed to gain at least five pounds over the next year, or else he would need a feeding tube placement to assist his weight gain. I was familiar with a feeding tube as a nurse; however, it was something I hoped to avoid.

After that visit, we fought for every pound he gained. He'd consume milkshakes with added protein, *Pediasure* for the extra calories, avocados for healthy fats, and starchy high-calorie snacks. We centered our world around his diet, all for him. I came up with creative ways to keep his diet varied and fun for him. Lincoln had to fight extra hard to grow since birth. His body had to heal an open wound, and the pressure of his Omphalocele caused him to breathe faster than most infants, so he burned calories more quickly. Even at rest, he was a calorie-burning machine. Eventually, he started to gain again and put on seven beautiful pounds that year.

Lincoln qualified for physical therapy at home for some right-sided weakness and torticollis to strengthen his neck muscles. He was discharged very quickly from physical therapy after we got home. Because we saw no improvement in his head control, we eventually found an outpatient physical therapist for those issues for a second opinion, and he preferred to tilt his head to the left instead of upright. He hated his tummy time more than a normal infant because of his stomach. Even when we forced him to do it to help strengthen his neck, he was so weak and tired that we couldn't continue it for long enough to gain the strength he needed in his neck muscles.

He completed six weeks of physical therapy, focusing on strengthening his core and neck muscles. During those visits, I struggled to watch him fight through the sessions. I internalized the pain he felt and felt it, too. I strived to advocate for his care and to be his voice until he had his own.

There were bright spots that first year. He no longer needed to see cardiology (heart) specialists after he was four months old because his atrial septal defect was minimal. We wouldn't have to follow up on it until he was three years old. At that age, they would be able to decide whether to operate and close the hole in the wall of his heart if needed or if it would be completely resolved with no medical intervention. We stopped needing nephrology (kidney) specialists by six months of age because his hydronephrosis cleared up on its own.

We continued to meet with his surgical team every six months until they decided the visits could be reduced to once per year. The surgical department is going to be a part of Lincoln's life until he's an adult due to the number of complications that he may face, though I pray that never occurs.

Every time a specialist signed off on his care, I cried tears of joy for our son and tears tinged with sadness for the children who still needed them. I had a soft spot for other parents going through struggles like ours. I continued to pray for good news, not just for our son but for all medically complex children.

I look at our son and am amazed at his resilient strength. He seemed unaware that any part of his care was not how it was supposed to be. Every time he needed bloodwork or had to be restrained for imaging, he'd cry for a bit, then quickly recover. Some of the procedures seem to be harder on Dylan and me than Lincoln. I can only hope he doesn't remember anything during this time. I knew he was strong, and here he was, continually proving the fact.

"I want to tell you everything I know, carry, and guide you. Yet somehow, as your tiny finger points to things in wonder and your eyes meet mine, the paradigm shifts. I once thought I was to show you the world when all along you came to show me."

-Jessica Urlichs

CHAPTER 27

Miles and Miles of Milestones

Our first night home was one I'll never forget. When we got home, my mother was there waiting on our porch. I wanted nothing more than to hug her and show her Lincoln. She had tears in her eyes as she hugged me. I'll never forget her face when she saw him. It was a mixture of joy and relief.

We asked for privacy at first in order to ease into the house. I needed to pump and feed Lincoln right away due to the long car ride. Our living room was full of gifts, but I was too overwhelmed and drained to notice. My main concern was feeding Lincoln.

My dad arrived a few hours later. He seemed proud to be meeting his first grandson. Both of my parents were reserved around Lincoln, fearing he was fragile and not wanting to do anything to hurt him. They loved him and us so much, and I was grateful they were there. I needed their embrace in every way. Dylan's family decided to meet Lincoln the day after we got home.

The first night was emotional and sleepless. Being new parents without the support of a team of medical professionals at our disposal was terrifying. I missed my bed, sure, but I also wanted the security of the hospital alarms that would ensure Lincoln was well.

We attempted a bassinet that connected to our bed for him to sleep in. I don't think I slept more than two hours that night. The bassinet ended up being too small for Lincoln because he was used to being in a spacious crib at the hospital. His first sleeping arrangement at home lasted eight days before we relocated him to his crib across the hall. He made that crib look giant, and he was finally able to settle in more comfortably there.

My mom stayed with us the first night. She didn't say much but didn't have to – her presence meant the world to me and, in a way, made me feel safer than having an entire team of medical professionals outside the door.

Throughout the night, when Lincoln awoke, Dylan warmed up the bottles, and I pumped while I fed the baby. My mom got to see firsthand the projectile vomit every time our son ate that night. I braced myself before each episode, but I wasn't used to it yet. Every time he threw up, I cried. My mom seemed cautious around Lincoln. We all had new realities to adjust to. In the subsequent days, Dylan and I learned the dance of marriage with the newly added steps of parenthood.

During those first six months, we mastered Lincoln's feedings, learned how to handle his vomiting, and got into the rhythm of doctor's visits and the rest of his care. Lincoln's sac of organs took up around ninety percent of his abdomen, and everything all but returned inside his little belly in three months.

I was able to be out of work for six months. During those months, my confidence in being not just a competent mother but a good mother skyrocketed. There was not a day I can recall where it all "clicked" for me, and being a mom just worked out. It was baptism by fire.

We adapted to Lincoln's sleep routine as well. If he was awake, so were we. He was a terrible sleeper for the first four months, waking every two to three hours to eat. Dylan and I had to learn to function on a handful of hours of broken sleep. After six weeks, Dylan had to return to work. While he did his best to help me, I preferred he slept so that he would be able to drive and work safely.

When they say everything changes once you have a baby, take it in the most literal sense. I never changed as much in such a short time as I did during the time of my pregnancy and Lincoln's first year of life. But one thing is certain: I am grateful that I did.

"Let me mother out of my best hopes
instead of my worst fear."

– Sarah Bessey

EPILOGUE

Lincoln's First Surgery

We spent our first Christmas as a family of three at home, isolating ourselves for our son's first surgery, which took place on December 28th, 2020.

Our first Christmas together was incredibly special to us in the oddest of ways – it was just Dylan, Lincoln, and me. FaceTiming our family that Christmas wasn't easy. It felt like another item on a long list of not getting what I envisioned being a family looked like.

The surgeon felt comfortable operating when Lincoln was just five months old instead of waiting until the usual twelve-plus months. We agreed that we would get through the holidays, and around seven-and-a-half months, we would have the operation done. Lincoln weighed right under twenty pounds, which gave him an advantage. The earlier we could get his stomach repaired, the better it was for his development.

The plan for this procedure was to take the contents of his Omphalocele and put them back in the abdominal cavity. At the same time, they had to piece together his core to make it sturdy enough to close him up.

The sac that had his liver and intestines stuck out two to three inches in depth and was about four inches wide. Any time you applied pressure to it, it would sink into his belly. The excess in the bulge saddled him with extra weight and prevented him from crawling.

We agreed with the surgeon that this procedure needed to take place for him to continue developing. It took multiple therapeutic modalities to get him strong enough, big enough, and to a place where he had enough space in his abdomen to operate.

As scary as it was to watch our son go into his first surgery, we were glad to move forward with this procedure. There was a morbid sense in the back of my mind that the procedure wouldn't end well, but I kept it at the back of my mind because I felt the benefits outweighed the risks. This surgery would ultimately be life-ending or life-saving.

On the day of his surgery, we took videos and pictures together as we waited for the surgical team to wheel Lincoln into the operating room. He looked adorable, dressed in a tiny surgical gown, just sucking away at his thumb, trying to get whatever food he could from it since he couldn't eat.

The mother in me wished for the closeness of him in my arms and to breastfeed him one last time that day. I wanted to provide some comfort for him, and I honestly needed some comfort myself.

The prep time for his surgery ended when a man in a drawn-on, cat-themed mask came to take him to the operating room.

We consented to the procedure and watched him roll away into the care of the team.

I wanted one more minute with him and approximately five hundred more kisses. I kept praying we would see our little boy again. I knew this surgery was going to improve his life, and I was excited about the miracle of modern medicine. I had a sinking pit in my stomach during the wait. The only choice I had at the moment was to trust the team and God to bring him back to us again.

We made our way to the cafeteria to get some food while we waited. I recall looking down at my fingertips in the elevator on the way there. The ink where they marked Lincoln's surgical sites got on me. I even took a picture of it to remind myself what a resilient child we had. I also felt the stinging realization that a child shouldn't have to be resilient from such a young age. I shed some tears in the elevator and hugged Dylan tightly.

Lincoln's surgery ran longer than anticipated as they additionally repaired his bilateral inguinal hernias – hernias on both sides of his groin area.

We reunited with him after more than five hours of waiting. The surgeon told us that everything went great, but I remember sensing some exhaustion in her demeanor. She was cautiously confident that Lincoln wouldn't have complications and that he wouldn't require any follow-up surgeries. She even crossed her own fingers in gesture, saying that she was hopeful this would be all surgery-wise. She reviewed the potential surgical complications and explained that our son had lots of scar tissue. She also noticed during the procedure that his liver had scar tissue that appeared to be wrapped up around and near it as his body's way of pulling the liver in the Omphalocele sac back into place where it should be. She was also pleasantly surprised that his abdominal cavity had the exact amount of space needed to fit the organs into place. She appeared to be almost as gratified as Dylan and I were that everything went so well. My mind immediately went to God, and I thanked Him. We were ecstatic that everything went as well as it could.

I had to wait for the team to clean our son up and for the anesthesia to wear off a bit more before seeing him. Dylan had to wait until we got to his hospital room. Both of us sat in the waiting room on the surgical unit until they turned the lights off.

After what felt like another lifetime, they called me to see him. I remember running to the PACU, where he was recovering, and still feeling like my feet weren't going fast enough. I was shaking uncontrollably, and my hands were as cold as ice.

I anticipated seeing Lincoln's new flat belly and the artificial belly button they gave to him but braced myself to watch him endure the pain of recovery.

Seeing his belly after surgery was something I'll never forget. They had to cut from just below Lincoln's sternum, almost down to his groin. As much as we did to prepare for this day, it still wasn't easy to see him so vulnerable.

I felt an overwhelming sense in that moment that we made it – that this was worth all the struggle. I vividly recall saying out loud to the nurse, "Wow, just look at him, look at that belly, that flat belly." She held my hand and told me he was one of the healthiest Omphalocele babies she had ever encountered. He survived the closure surgery and was just one more hospital stay away from being healthy and thriving. He defied the odds at just seven-and-a-half months old and nineteen-and-a-half pounds.

December 28th, 2023

Three years ago, today was the scariest day of our lives, aside from receiving the diagnosis. We had to hand over our 7.5-month-old and pray that he would have a successful surgery. It was a feat to get through the emotions of the day. His life leading up to that day placed us in situations where we were forced to confront our fears. We had to go through it; there was no way around it. His surgery was just another milestone that we prayed to reach and get through. He was on the younger side for a Giant Omphalocele repair surgery, and that was a concern for me, but looking back, he was ready for it. I am grateful we complied and had it done because he took off like a rocket the very next day, hitting milestone after milestone.

That same black and white blob I studied intensely for months became a lanky newborn once wrapped in gauze and draped with tubes and is now the wittiest three-and-a-half-year-old that just ran up to Dylan and me in his usual shirtless fashion. Seeing the scars on his belly sting a little less these days reminds me of how we have won all the battles we have faced so far.

We stand hugging in the kitchen, and Lincoln weasels himself between us before looking up to say, "Guys, oh no, you don't! Don't forget me!" He says it so innocently, and for a moment, we are just us three like we were from the start a few years back. I smile, thinking how cute it is that he could ever think either of us could forget him.

He is everything I dreamed he would be and more. He is truly my Lucky Lincoln. The one who kickstarts my morning and who I look forward to seeing once I return home from work.

December 28th, 2023

We end our nights together with the affirmation: "You are big, brave, and strong. Always." He joins in with each word of it or sometimes chimes in for the end, yelling, "ALWAYS!"

He is unique because of his life story, and yet he is so much more than his medical chart. I will spend the rest of my life being his best advocate and biggest fan. Lincoln will always be my greatest blessing and the very best part of me.

"Life has a way of wrecking what you think you want by daring you to show up to your challenges."

- Shelbi Zimmerman

ACKNOWLEDGMENTS

I grew an understanding of my mother, one I previously did not have access to. I reminisced on the sacrifices she made for her children. I related to her in this new and beautiful way. This understanding was instantaneous and personal. I gained a new respect for other mothers, but especially my own. She was a reliable support and light throughout my pregnancy and a sounding board for all my concerns. She returned my fears with her comfort, and I love her for that.

I relied on my Aunt Penny as well. She didn't brush my fears off when I confided in her well before we got the diagnosis. She texted me one day, telling me to believe in myself and to trust in God. She was always a text or call away. She tried to keep me positive but always had room for the deep level of concern built into my day-to-day life.

My sisters, Chelcee and Erika, and my sister-in-law, Alexis, helped me so much as well. Each had their ways of helping out. I equally needed them.

My younger sister, Erika, sent me a text message on my birthday that I still have on my phone years later. It said, "Happy Birthday, Shelbi, I love you so, so much! I hope you have a great day! You're so, so strong, and I'm proud of how you're handling this. You're going to be the BEST mom in the world!!" Her words strengthened my belief in myself, and I hold onto that because of her.

My older sister, Chelcee, was the first person I confided in when we learned the news. She was the first person I hugged when I got to our parent's house. She held me together at times – that is just who she is. She probably doesn't realize what a large role she had in keeping me together. She allowed me to vent about all my fears and didn't shy away from suggesting I seek a therapist if I needed to. She has always been a great older sister to me, showing her love in many ways. She included me on outings with my niece because she knew that even on my darkest and most challenging days, it would put a smile on my face.

From the beginning, I chose my sister-in-law, Alexis, as the god-mother to our son. I trusted her unwavering belief that she inherited from her mother to be a source of light during my pregnancy. I knew without a doubt that both she and her mother would be right beside me if I ever asked them to.

My mother-in-law, Gina, was a stalwart of optimism. You could not get that woman to indulge in a negative thought throughout my pregnancy if you tried. She had good reason to be positive, too. She prayed very hard for us. What she granted to me was the faith I needed when mine was lost. It was the greatest gift to me. I will always cherish her for that.

Our medical team was more than just a medical team. They will take up space in my heart for a lifetime. Each and every person who saw me appointment after appointment played a large role in my life during my pregnancy. They were there to reassure me after every ultrasound, local or at the other hospital and celebrated each week as if we had made it through together. I owe each of them a big thanks.

Dr. Christina, who delivered the news of our son's diagnosis, will always be well-remembered. She was our maternal-fetal medicine doctor and was the one with the facts. She encouraged and reinforced me to make it to my due date. She gave me the strength to believe in myself. She believed in our son, too.

These medical professionals who didn't owe us any more of their time went as far as sharing their phone numbers with us so that we could text our questions. When we found out she could follow our care from the small town where we lived into the bigger hospital in Pittsburgh, it was a victory I was desperate for. I consider her a living angel.

A nurse who became my friend, Mary, was always there for me, checking in and sending her love. I called her first when I missed my period. I called later when I started to bleed heavily during my pregnancy. She reminded me I could do this. She was more than a nurse to me.

Nicole K. was the only ultrasound tech I trusted to see during the pregnancy. She took great care of me. We saw each other weekly at the end of the pregnancy. The grace she showed us on the day of the diagnosis helped in ways I'm still processing. She understood the mental load of what we faced and kept her smile. She encouraged us that he did look healthy otherwise. She was compassionate when bad news came and embraced us through the better news. My pregnancy would have been entirely different without her- I am also glad you have met Lincoln. I prayed for that day so very hard.

Jessica, you have been the one to hear my hopes and fears surrounding this book process, and I am blessed to learn and unlearn all the things with your guidance. You touch a lot of lives, and I'm glad you have touched mine. Thanks for believing in me.

And last but certainly not least, Dylan. I could go on and on about you and list out just how much you mean to me, but I hope that through reading this book, you get a glimpse of how much I value you. Without you, I would not be the woman I am today nor the mother I am. You have shown me immense support and grace, and most importantly, you have shown me true love. I truly, without a doubt, know that I could not have survived my pregnancy with Lincoln without you by my side, and I know God hand-picked you for me. We are blessed to spend this life together, and what we have had throughout the hardest of trials is our unbreakable bond. We have what we have fought for. The last ten years have been filled with so much love. So thank you for being you. I love you forever, kid.

INDEX

1"Facts about Omphalocele." Center for Disease Control and Prevention. 28 June 2023. https://www.cdc.gov/ncbddd/birthdefects/omphalocele.html.

2"Data & Statistics on Birth Defects." Center for Disease Control and Prevention. 28 June 2023. https://www.cdc.gov/ncbddd/birthdefects/data.html.

3Everlast. "What It's Like," Whitney Ford Sings the Blues. Irving Music, Inc., 8 September 1998. https://www.youtube.com/watch?v=qA1nGPM9yHA.

4Daigle, Lauren. "Look Up Child," Look Up Child. Centricity Music, 7 September 2018. https://www.youtube.com/watch?v=7NAYz0zh_Es.

5Heller, J. J. "Missing Peace," Missing Peace. David Heller, JJ Heller, and Andy Gullahorn, 11 January 2020. https://www.youtube.com/watch?v=2Or4e7mu5Uw.

FOR FURTHER REFERENCE

For additional research and support, please visit the following sources:

UCSF Health (https://www.ucsfhealth.org/)

March of Dimes (https://www.marchofdimes.org/)

MOO -- Mothers Of Omphaloceles (https://www.facebook.com/groups/ompha-locele/)

Grady's Decision (https://www.gradysdecision.com)

MEET THE AUTHOR

Shelbi Zimmerman grew up in a typical small town in Pennsylvania where everything was predictable – just as she liked. The same year she got her dream job, she also married her "after" high school sweetheart. Right away, they began planning for their family. Everything was perfect until her journey through life took an unexpected turn when she faced the challenges of a high-risk pregnancy amid the chaos of a global pandemic.

In her professional life, Shelbi serves as a compassionate Licensed Practical Nurse, dedicating her skills to the well-being of students. However, it was her personal experience during a turbulent period that ignited a newfound passion within her: championing high-risk pregnant women. In addition to her role as a nurse, and advocate for high-risk mothers, Shelbi continues to cherish the joys of family life in Pennsylvania.

"Born For This: Embracing the Journey from High-Risk to Hopeful" is Shelbi's debut novel. You can learn more about Shelbi by following her on social media.